THE Young Chef's

COOKBOOK:
A BEGINNER'S GUIDE TO FUN AND SIMPLE COOKING

Empower Young Minds in the Kitchen with Easy, Nutritious Recipes and Essential Cooking Skills

SIMON AMPORT

Copyright © 2024 Simon Amport.

All rights reserved.

No part of this publication may be reproduced, distributed or transmitted in any form or by any means, including photocopying, recording or other electronic or mechanical methods, without the prior written permission of the publisher, except in the case of brief quotations, reviews and other noncommercial uses permitted by copyright law.

Contents

Introduction

Alright, gather 'round, young chefs! Let me tell you a quick story. My name is Simon and I am a chef. I am also the oldest of six in my family, so I have a few younger eyes looking up at me. My younger brothers wanted to cook in the kitchen and be just like me, but the recipes were too challenging and complicated. That is why I decided to create the Young Chef Cookbook! Pretty soon, my younger brothers went from saying, "I can't do this" to "What can I cook next?" That's the magic of easy recipes and a bit of confidence.

And that's what "The Young Chef Cookbook" is all about! This book is here to help you, kids and teens, take charge in the kitchen with super easy snacks and meals. No need to be scared or think you can't cook. These recipes are simple, fun, and will make you feel like a pro in no time. Whether you want to whip up a quick snack after school or cook a meal for your family, you've got this!

What makes this book stand out? First off, the recipes are super simple and easy to follow. No complicated steps or fancy kitchen gadgets needed. We use common ingredients that you probably already have at home. Plus, I've sprinkled in some modern slang and fun lingo to keep things interesting and relatable. Cooking should be fun, not stressful, right?

Hey there, you! Yes, you, the one reading this introduction. I want you to know that this book is designed especially for you. Think of it as your first step into the wonderful world of cooking. The steps are clear, there's no confusing culinary language, and each recipe is crafted to be fun and easy. So, get ready to embark on a culinary adventure!

Let me introduce myself. I'm someone who genuinely loves helping kids and teens overcome cooking challenges. I've seen firsthand how empowering it is for young people to gain confidence in the kitchen. I've dedicated a lot of time to creating recipes that are not just easy to follow, but also delicious and fun to make. My goal is to provide guidance that's reputable and easy to follow, so you can feel confident every step of the way.

Here's a sneak peek at what's inside "The Young Chef Cookbook." We've got a variety of recipes that cover everything from breakfast to dinner, and snacks to desserts. You'll find sections on party foods that will make you the star of any gathering. And there are cooking challenges that are designed to be both fun and rewarding. Each chapter is packed with tasty recipes that will make you want to jump into the kitchen and start cooking.

Now, I want to leave you with a bit of encouragement. Jump in and start cooking! Don't be afraid to make mistakes. Remember, even the best chefs had to start somewhere. Cooking is a fun, creative, and incredibly rewarding activity. It's not just about making food; it's about expressing yourself and having fun along the way. So, grab your apron, pick a recipe, and let's get cooking!

So, what are you waiting for? Flip the page, pick a recipe, and let's make some magic in the kitchen together. The adventure starts now!

CHAPTER 1

Getting Started in the Kitchen

Alright, young chefs, let's get this show on the road! Have you ever watched a cooking show and thought, "That looks fun, but I could never do that"? Well, guess what? You totally can! I remember when my little brother Jude, who's just 11, came into the kitchen one afternoon. He was nervous about even boiling water. But after we went over some basic kitchen safety and simple techniques, he made the fluffiest pancakes ever. His confidence skyrocketed, and he couldn't wait to try cooking more recipes. So, let's make sure you're ready to tackle any recipe with ease and safety. This chapter is all about getting you comfortable in the kitchen, starting with the most important thing—safety.

1.1 KITCHEN SAFETY 101

Kitchen safety is your first step to becoming a confident and skilled young chef. Think of it as your foundation. Without it, even the simplest recipe can turn into a disaster. So, let's dive into the basics. First off, always wash your hands before you start cooking. It's not just about keeping things clean; it's about keeping you and anyone who eats your food safe from germs. Wear an apron to protect your clothes and tie back long hair to keep it out of your face and food. These little steps set you up for success.

Now, let's talk about adult supervision. If you're just starting out, it's a good idea to have an adult nearby. They can help you with tricky steps and make sure you're staying safe, especially when you're using heat or knives. Trust me, even the best chefs started with a little help from someone more experienced.

Fire and heat safety are crucial when you're in the kitchen. Always use oven mitts or potholders when handling hot pots, pans, or baking trays. Burns are no joke, and a simple mitt can save you from a lot of pain. When using the stove, make sure the handles of your pots and pans are turned inward. This prevents accidental bumps that could cause hot food to spill. Remember, never leave the kitchen unattended when something is cooking, especially if you're using the stove or oven. If a fire does start—don't panic. Know where the fire extinguisher is and how to use it. If the fire is small, like a grease fire, you can often smother it with a lid or baking soda. But if it's larger, get out of the kitchen and call for help immediately.

Knives can be a bit scary, but with the right techniques, they don't have to be. Always use a proper grip on the knife, holding the handle firmly with your fingers wrapped around it. Use the "claw" method to keep your fingers safe. This means curling your fingers under and holding the food with your knuckles facing the knife. This way, if the knife slips, it hits your knuckles and not your fingertips. When you're done, store knives in a safe place, like a knife block or a drawer with a knife guard, to keep them and you safe.

Hygiene and cleanliness are equally important. Wash your hands before and after handling food, especially raw meat or eggs. Cleaning up spills immediately prevents slips and keeps the cooking area safe. Always wash fruits and vegetables thoroughly to remove any dirt or pesticides. A clean kitchen isn't just nicer to work in—it's safer, too.

So, young chefs, remember that safety is your best friend in the kitchen. Master these basics, and you'll be ready to tackle any recipe with confidence and ease. Now, let's get cooking!

1.2 ESSENTIAL TOOLS AND GADGETS FOR YOUNG CHEFS

Alright, now that we're all set on kitchen safety, let's talk about the tools you'll need. Every chef, no matter how young, needs the right tools to create their culinary masterpieces. Think of these as your kitchen superpowers. First up, we have measuring cups and spoons. These are crucial for getting your recipes just right. Imagine trying to make cookies without measuring the flour or sugar. You'd either have a soupy mess or rock-hard dough. Measuring cups come in different sizes for dry ingredients, while liquid measuring cups usually have a spout and lines to show measurements. Measuring spoons are for smaller quantities like baking powder or vanilla extract. Always level off dry ingredients with a flat edge for accuracy.

Next, let's talk about mixing bowls. These are your go-to for combining ingredients. You'll need them for everything from mixing batter to tossing a salad. They come in various sizes, and having a set of at least three different sizes is a good idea. Stainless-steel bowls are durable and easy to clean, while glass bowls let you see the ingredients better. Whisks and spatulas are also essential. A whisk is perfect for beating eggs or mixing dry ingredients to get rid of lumps. On the other hand, spatulas are great for scraping down the sides of a bowl or folding ingredients together gently. Each tool has a specific job, and using the right one makes cooking much easier and more fun.

Now, let's highlight some kid-friendly gadgets. Safe, kid-friendly knives are a must. These are usually smaller, with rounded tips and grips designed for smaller hands. They're sharp enough to cut through food, but not so sharp that they're dangerous. Non-slip cutting boards are another great tool. They stay put while you're chopping, reducing the chance of accidents. Easy-to-use can openers can also be a lifesaver— no more struggling with those stubborn lids. These gadgets are designed to make cooking safer and more enjoyable for young chefs like you.

But having the right tools isn't just about using them; it's also about taking care of them. Proper maintenance ensures your tools last longer and stay safe to use. Always clean your tools right after using them. Mixing bowls, measuring cups, and spatulas should be washed with warm, soapy water and dried thoroughly to prevent any bacteria buildup. Store your tools in an organized manner. For instance, keep all your measuring spoons together on a ring or in a drawer, and store knives in a knife block or on a magnetic strip. This not only keeps your kitchen tidy but also makes it easier to find what you need when you're cooking.

Sharpening knives is also important, but it should always be done with adult supervision. A dull knife is more dangerous than a sharp one because it requires more force to cut, increasing the risk of slipping. Most kitchens have a knife sharpener or honing rod, and learning to use these tools can keep your knives in good shape. Remember, well-maintained tools make your cooking experience smoother and more enjoyable.

So, there you have it. With the right tools and gadgets, you're well on your way to becoming a confident, skilled young chef. These essentials will make your time in the kitchen easier and more fun. Now, let's roll up those sleeves, gather your tools, and start cooking!

I.3 BASIC COOKING TECHNIQUES EXPLAINED

Hey there, young chefs! Now that you're familiar with kitchen safety and have your tools ready, it's time to learn some fundamental cooking techniques. Think of these as the building blocks of cooking. Master these, and you'll be able to handle any recipe with confidence. Let's start with stirring and mixing. These may seem simple, but doing them right makes a huge difference in how your food turns out. When mixing ingredients for something like cake batter, use a whisk or spatula to combine them smoothly. Start by adding your dry ingredients to your wet ones and stir gently to avoid splashing. Hold the bowl steady with one hand while you mix with the other. This keeps your ingredients from spilling out and making a mess. Remember, the goal is to blend everything evenly without over-mixing, which can make your batter tough.

Next up is chopping and slicing. This is where you can really feel like a chef. Hold your knife with a firm grip, and use the "claw" method to keep your fingers safe. Curl your fingers under and let your knuckles guide the knife. When slicing something like a carrot, start by cutting it into manageable pieces. Lay the flat side down to keep it stable, then slice it into even rounds. Want to know a neat trick? Use a rocking motion with your knife, starting at the tip and rocking back to the handle. This helps you slice smoothly without having to press down hard. Practice makes perfect, so don't get discouraged if your pieces aren't perfectly even at first.

Boiling and simmering are next on our list. These techniques are essential for preparing a variety of dishes, from pasta to soups. To boil pasta, fill a large pot with water and bring it to a rolling boil over high heat. Add a generous pinch of salt—it helps flavor the pasta as it cooks. Once the water is boiling, add your pasta and stir it occasionally to prevent sticking. Cook it according to the package instructions, usually around 8–10 minutes, until it's al dente, or firm to the bite. Drain the pasta in a colander and give it a quick rinse with warm water if you're not using it immediately.

Simmering is a gentler cooking method, perfect for soups and stews. Once you've brought your liquid to a boil, reduce the heat to low or medium-low so that small bubbles rise to the surface slowly. This keeps your ingredients tender and allows flavors to meld together beautifully. For example, if you're making a vegetable soup, bring your broth to a boil first, then add your veggies and reduce the heat to a simmer. Let it cook until the vegetables are tender but not mushy, usually about 20–30 minutes.

Let's break these down into easy steps. For boiling pasta, start by filling a large pot with water and placing it on the stove over high heat. Add salt and wait for the water to boil. Once boiling, add the pasta and stir occasionally. Cook for the recommended time, then drain and rinse. For mixing ingredients, gather your tools and ingredients. Begin by combining your dry ingredients in one bowl and wet ingredients in another. Slowly add the dry to the wet while stirring gently with a whisk or spatula. For chopping and slicing, grip your knife properly and use the "claw" method to keep your fingers safe. Use a rocking motion to slice your ingredients evenly. For simmering, bring your liquid to a boil, then reduce the heat and let it cook slowly.

Visual aids can make these techniques even clearer. Imagine a photo showing the correct way to hold a knife or a step-by-step series of images demonstrating the boiling process. These visuals can guide you and ensure you're doing things correctly. It's like having a mini cooking class right in your kitchen!

Remember, mastering these techniques takes time and practice. Start with simple recipes to build your confidence. Patience and persistence are key. Cooking isn't about getting everything perfect the first time; it's about learning and improving with each dish you make. So, don't be afraid to make mistakes. Every great chef started exactly where you are now. Keep practicing, stay patient, and most importantly, have fun with it!

1.4 UNDERSTANDING MEASUREMENTS AND INGREDIENTS

Hey there, young chefs! Let's talk about something super important in cooking and baking—measurements. Accurate measurements are crucial because they ensure your recipes turn out just right. Imagine trying to bake cookies without measuring the sugar or flour. You might end up with a gooey mess or rock-hard dough. Knowing how to measure ingredients properly gives you consistent results and makes your food taste delicious every time.

First, let's discuss the difference between liquid and dry measuring cups. They're designed differently for a reason. Liquid measuring cups usually have a spout and measurement lines on the side. They're perfect for ingredients like water, milk, and oil. Dry measuring cups, on the other hand, are meant for ingredients like flour, sugar, and cocoa powder. They come in sets, usually ranging from a quarter cup to a full cup. Using the right type of measuring cup ensures you get the correct amount of each ingredient, which is key to making your recipes turn out as expected.

When measuring dry ingredients, it's important to level them off. Scoop your ingredient into the measuring cup, then use a flat edge, like the back of a knife, to scrape off the excess. This gives you an accurate measurement. For small quantities, measuring spoons are your best friend. They're great for ingredients like baking powder, salt, and vanilla extract. Make sure to level off dry ingredients in measuring spoons, just like you do with cups. This attention to detail can make a big difference in your cooking and baking.

Measuring liquids correctly is just as important. When using a liquid measuring cup, place it on a flat surface and check the measurement at eye level. This helps you avoid overpouring or underpouring. If you're measuring something thick like honey or syrup, use a dry measuring cup and level it off with a spatula. This ensures you're getting the exact amount needed for your recipe. Accuracy in measurements can be the difference between a cake that rises perfectly and one that falls flat.

Let's familiarize ourselves with some common ingredients you'll encounter frequently. Basic pantry staples include flour, sugar, salt, baking powder, and baking soda. These are the building blocks for many recipes. For fresh ingredients, you'll often use eggs, milk, butter, and various fruits and vegetables. Knowing what these ingredients look like and how they behave in recipes helps you understand why they're used and how to substitute them if needed.

Speaking of substitutions, let's tackle allergies. It's common to have allergies or dietary restrictions, but that doesn't mean you can't enjoy delicious food. For example, if you're allergic to eggs, you can use applesauce or mashed bananas as a substitute in baking. If you're dairy-free, plant-based milks like almond or soy can replace regular milk. Identifying potential allergens in recipes is crucial. Always check the ingredient list and know what substitutions work best for your needs.

Imagine you're about to bake a batch of brownies but realize you're out of eggs. No need to panic! Simply use a quarter cup of applesauce for each egg. This not only solves your problem but also adds a unique flavor to your brownies.

Understanding these substitutions makes you a versatile chef, ready to tackle any recipe with what you have on hand.

Accurate measurements and knowing your ingredients are the backbone of successful cooking and baking. They ensure your dishes turn out delicious and consistent every time. As you get more comfortable with these basics, you'll find that experimenting with different ingredients and substitutions becomes second nature. So, grab your measuring cups and spoons, and let's create some outstanding dishes together!

1.5 KEEPING IT CLEAN: EASY KITCHEN CLEANUP TIPS

Alright, young chefs, let's face it – cooking can be messy. But keeping a clean kitchen is super important, and it's not just about making things look nice. A clean kitchen keeps you safe and healthy. When you cook, you're dealing with different types of food, and if you're not careful, bacteria from raw meat can end up on your veggies or clean dishes. This is called cross-contamination, and it can make you and your family sick. Also, a clean kitchen helps keep pests like ants and roaches away. They love crumbs and leftover food, so cleaning up right away is key.

Now, let's go through a step-by-step guide on how to clean up after cooking. First, start with the dishes and utensils you used. Fill the sink with warm, soapy water and let the dishes soak for a few minutes. This helps loosen any food stuck on them. Then, use a sponge or dishcloth to scrub each item clean. Rinse them thoroughly and place them in a drying rack or dry them with a clean towel. Don't forget to wash pots and pans, too. If something is really stuck on, fill it with some warm water and let it soak while you clean the rest of the kitchen.

Next, wipe down countertops and surfaces. Use a clean cloth or paper towel with a bit of kitchen cleaner or a mixture of water and a splash of vinegar. This helps remove any food particles and grease. Pay attention to areas where you prepared raw meat, and give those spots an excellent scrub to prevent any bacteria from spreading. Don't forget to wipe down the stove and any other surfaces you used. A clean workspace not only looks good but also makes it easier to cook the next time you're in the kitchen.

Here are some quick cleanup hacks to make the process faster and easier. One trick is to soak pots and pans immediately after using them. This prevents food from sticking and makes them much easier to clean later. For tough stains, try using a mixture of baking soda and vinegar. Sprinkle some baking soda on the stain, add a bit of vinegar, and let it fizz. After a few minutes, scrub it clean. This works great on stubborn spots and leaves your kitchen sparkling. Another hack is to keep a small trash bowl nearby while you cook. Toss scraps and peelings into the bowl, and when you're done, just empty it into the trash. This keeps your workspace tidy and makes cleanup a breeze.

Cleaning up doesn't have to be a solo job. Sharing cleanup duties can make the process faster and even fun. Divide tasks among family members or friends who helped with the cooking. One person can handle the dishes while another wipes down the counters. Making cleanup a part of your cooking routine helps everyone take responsibility for their mess. It's a great way to build teamwork and ensures that the kitchen stays clean and ready for the next cooking adventure.

For example, after a big family dinner, everyone pitches in. Dad washes the dishes, Mom dries and puts them away, and you wipe down the counters and sweep the floor. In no time, the kitchen is spotless, and you all get to relax and enjoy the rest of the evening together. Sharing the work not only makes it go faster but also teaches everyone the importance of working together and keeping a clean space.

So, young chefs, remember that a clean kitchen is a happy kitchen. It keeps you safe, makes cooking more enjoyable, and ensures that you're ready for the next delicious recipe you want to try. Cleaning up might not be the most fun part of cooking, but with these tips and a bit of teamwork, it can be quick and easy. Keep these tips in mind, and you'll always have a clean, safe kitchen to cook in. Now, let's get ready for the next exciting part of our culinary adventure!

CHAPTER 2

Breakfast Bonanza

Alright, young chefs, imagine waking up on a bright, sunny morning with the smell of something delicious wafting through the house. You rub your eyes and head to the kitchen, only to find your older brother, Alex, making the most vibrant and colorful breakfast you've ever seen. He's whipping up a smoothie bowl, and the kitchen counter is covered with bowls of fresh fruits, nuts, and seeds. You watch as he blends up a creamy smoothie base, pours it into a bowl, and then starts decorating it with an artistic flair. It looks like a masterpiece, and you can't wait to dig in. That's the magic of smoothie bowls – they're not just a treat for your taste buds but also a feast for your eyes.

DIY SMOOTHIE BOWLS

So, what exactly is a smoothie bowl? Imagine a smoothie that's so thick and creamy, you can eat it with a spoon. Sounds amazing, right? Smoothie bowls are a fun and healthy breakfast option that packs a punch of nutrition and flavor. They're like a blank canvas that you can decorate with all your favorite toppings. The best part? They're super versatile. Whether you're in the mood for something fruity, nutty, or chocolaty, you can customize your smoothie bowl to fit your taste.

Let's start with a basic smoothie bowl recipe that you can easily customize. The ingredients are simple: frozen berries, a ripe banana, yogurt, and milk or juice. First, grab your blender and toss in a cup and a half of frozen berries. You can use strawberries, blueberries, raspberries, or a mix of all three. Next, add one large banana. If you want an extra creamy texture, you can use a frozen banana. Now, add half a cup of yogurt. Greek yogurt works great because it's thick and adds a nice tangy flavor. Finally, pour in about half a cup of milk or juice. You can use regular milk, almond milk, or even orange juice for a citrusy twist. Blend everything until smooth and creamy, then pour it into a bowl.

Now comes the fun part — the toppings! This is where you can get really creative and make your smoothie bowl unique and colorful. Start with some fresh fruits like kiwi, mango, and strawberries. Slice them up and arrange them on top of your smoothie base. Next, add some crunch with nuts and seeds. Chia seeds, almonds, and granola are all great options. Not only do they add texture, but they also boost the nutritional value of your bowl. For a touch of fun, sprinkle on some coconut flakes or cacao nibs. These extras not only taste great but also make your bowl look like a work of art.

When it comes to arranging your toppings, think like an artist. You can create patterns with fruit slices, like a spiral of kiwi or a fan of strawberry slices. Play with different colors and textures to make your bowl visually appealing. For example, place bright yellow mango next to dark purple berries for a striking contrast. You can even try making shapes or letters with your toppings. The possibilities are endless, and the result is not only delicious but also Instagram-worthy.

Here's a little tip: the thicker your smoothie, the easier it is to keep your toppings from sinking. If your smoothie is too runny, add a bit more frozen fruit or a handful of ice cubes and blend again. You want the consistency to be thick enough to hold your toppings, but still smooth enough to eat with a spoon. Also, if you make extra smoothie, you can store it in the fridge for up to 24 hours or freeze it into popsicles for a refreshing treat later.

Smoothie bowls are not just a tasty breakfast; they're a celebration of flavors and colors. They're packed with vitamins, minerals, and antioxidants, making them a great way to start your day. Plus, they're a fun way to get creative in the kitchen. So, grab your blender, pick your favorite fruits, and let's make some smoothie magic happen!

OVERNIGHT OATS: NO-COOK BREAKFASTS

Imagine waking up and having breakfast ready to go – no cooking required. Overnight oats are like magic in a jar. They're the perfect solution for busy mornings when you're rushing to get ready for school or need a quick bite before heading out for soccer practice. Besides being super convenient, overnight oats are packed with fiber, which helps keep you full and energized throughout the morning. The best part? You can customize them in a million different ways to suit your taste. All you need is a little bit of prep the night before, and you'll have a delicious, nutritious breakfast waiting for you when you wake up.

Let's start with a basic overnight oats recipe. The ingredients are simple: rolled oats, milk or plant-based milk, yogurt, and a sweetener of your choice. Grab a mason jar or any container with a lid. Add half a cup of rolled oats to the jar. Pour in half a cup of milk – you can use regular milk, almond milk, or any other plant-based milk you like. Next, add a quarter cup of yogurt to make it creamy. If you like your oats a bit sweeter, stir in a tablespoon of honey, maple syrup, or agave. Give everything a good mix, seal the jar, and pop it in the fridge. By morning, the oats will have soaked up the liquid, becoming soft and ready to eat.

Now, let's make things interesting with some flavor variations. If you're a chocolate lover, try the Chocolate Peanut Butter variation. Mix in a tablespoon of cocoa powder and a spoonful of peanut butter before refrigerating. In the morning, add some banana slices on top for an extra treat. For a fruity twist, go for the Berry Blast version. Stir in a handful of mixed berries and a splash of vanilla extract, then drizzle a bit of honey over the top. If you're in the mood for something cozy, the Apple Cinnamon variation is perfect. Add a diced apple, a sprinkle of cinnamon, and a tablespoon of maple syrup. These flavors will make your oats taste like apple pie!

But don't stop there – you can experiment with your own favorite flavors and ingredients. Try adding nuts and seeds for some extra crunch. Chia seeds, flax seeds, and almonds are all great options that not only add texture but also boost the nutritional value of your oats. You can also play around with different types of milk. Coconut milk gives a tropical twist, while soy milk adds a bit of protein. The possibilities are endless, and each combination can bring a new and exciting taste to your breakfast.

Here's a little tip to make your overnight oats even more enjoyable: layer the ingredients. Start with a layer of oats, then add a layer of yogurt, followed by a layer of fruit, and repeat until your jar is full. This not only looks appealing but also ensures you get a bit of everything in each bite. If you like your oats thicker, reduce the amount of liquid, or if you prefer them more like a porridge, add a bit more milk.

Another great thing about overnight oats is that they can be made in advance and stored in the fridge for up to three days. This means you can prepare a few jars at once and have breakfast sorted for almost half the week. Imagine grabbing a jar of delicious overnight oats on a busy morning without having to think twice about what to eat. It's a game-changer!

So, grab your favorite jar, mix up some oats, and get creative with the flavors. Whether you stick to the basic recipe or venture into new combinations, you'll find that overnight oats are not just a quick breakfast solution, but also a fun way to start your day. Enjoy every spoonful, and don't be afraid to experiment with new ingredients to find your perfect mix.

FLUFFY PANCAKES WITH A TWIST

Imagine waking up on a lazy Saturday morning, the sun streaming through your window, and the delicious smell of pancakes filling the air. Pancakes are a classic breakfast that everyone loves, and the best part is they're super easy to make. Let's start with a foolproof pancake recipe that you can master in no time. You'll need some basic ingredients: flour, baking powder, milk, an egg, and butter. First, grab two bowls. In the first bowl, mix one cup of flour with two teaspoons of baking powder. In the second bowl, whisk together one cup of milk, one egg, and two tablespoons of melted butter. Now, pour the wet ingredients into the dry ingredients and mix until just combined. Don't worry if the batter is a bit lumpy; that's totally fine. Heat a griddle or non-stick pan over medium heat and lightly grease it with butter or oil. Pour a small ladle of batter onto the griddle and cook until bubbles form on the surface, then flip and cook until golden brown.

Now, let's get creative with some fun mix-ins and toppings to make your pancakes even more exciting. How about adding some chocolate chips to the batter for a sweet surprise in every bite? Or toss in a handful of fresh blueberries for a burst of fruity flavor. If you're feeling festive, sprinkle some colorful sprinkles into the batter to make funfetti pancakes that are sure to brighten anyone's day. When it comes to toppings, the sky's the limit. A dollop of whipped cream, a handful of fresh fruit, and a drizzle of syrup can turn a simple pancake into a breakfast masterpiece. You can even go savory with toppings like crispy bacon or a fried egg.

For those looking to try something a bit different, let's explore some specialty pancake variations. Banana pancakes are a delicious twist on the classic recipe. Simply mash a ripe banana and mix it into the batter. The banana adds natural sweetness and makes the pancakes extra fluffy. If you want to take your pancakes to the next level, try making rainbow pancakes. Divide your batter into several bowls and add a few drops of food coloring to each one. Cook each color separately, then stack them to create a rainbow stack that's as fun to look at as it is to eat.

Here are some tips to ensure your pancakes turn out fluffy and delicious every time. First, use a non-stick pan or griddle to prevent sticking and make flipping easier. Cook the pancakes over medium heat to avoid burning the outside, while the inside remains undercooked. You'll know it's time to flip the pancake when you see bubbles forming on the surface. Use a spatula to carefully flip it and cook until both sides are golden brown. If you're making a large batch, keep the cooked pancakes warm in the oven set to a low temperature while you finish cooking the rest.

Cooking pancakes can be a fun and rewarding experience, especially when you get creative with mix-ins and toppings. Whether you stick to the classic recipe or venture into new variations, you'll find that pancakes are a versatile and delicious breakfast option that everyone will love. So, grab your ingredients, heat up that griddle, and let's make some pancakes that will turn any morning into a special occasion.

2.4 BREAKFAST BURRITOS FOR ON-THE-GO

Picture this: you're running late for school, and you need a breakfast that's quick, tasty, and can be eaten on the go. Breakfast burritos are your perfect solution. They're like a whole meal wrapped up in a neat little package, easy to make and even easier to eat. Let's start with a basic recipe that you can whip up in no time. You'll need tortillas, scrambled eggs, and cheese. First, scramble a couple of eggs in a pan until they're fluffy and cooked through. Lay a tortilla flat on a plate, sprinkle some cheese on it, and then add the scrambled eggs. If you like, you can warm the tortilla in the microwave for a few seconds to make it more pliable. Roll it up tightly, and there you go – a simple, delicious breakfast burrito.

But why stop at just eggs and cheese? The beauty of breakfast burritos is that you can customize them to fit your taste. If you're a fan of protein, add some cooked bacon, sausage, or even tofu for a vegetarian option. For veggies, try adding bell peppers, spinach, or avocado. These not only add flavor but also pack in some extra nutrients. And don't forget the extras. A spoonful of salsa, a dollop of sour cream, or a splash of hot sauce can take your burrito to the next level. Each bite will be a burst of flavors, making your morning meal something to look forward to.

When it comes to wrapping and storing your burritos, it's all about keeping them fresh and easy to grab. If you're eating it right away, wrap it tightly in foil or parchment paper to keep everything together. This also makes it easy to eat on the go without making a mess. If you're making burritos in advance, wrap them individually in foil and store them in the refrigerator. They'll stay good for a few days, and you can just pop one in the microwave for a quick reheat. For longer storage, you can freeze them. Just wrap them in plastic wrap first, then in foil, and they'll be good for up to a month. Perfect for those mornings when you need something fast but satisfying.

Don't be afraid to get creative with your burrito fillings. Think about creating themed burritos that reflect different cuisines. For a Mexican-inspired burrito, add black beans, corn, and a bit of cumin to your eggs. Top it off with some fresh cilantro and a squeeze of lime. If you're in the mood for Mediterranean flavors, try adding some feta cheese, olives, and diced tomatoes. You can even throw in some quinoa for extra protein and texture. The possibilities are endless, and you can mix and match ingredients to find your perfect combination.

Here's a little tip to make your burritos even more fun: set up a burrito bar. Lay out all your fillings in separate bowls and let everyone build their own burrito. This is a great way to involve the whole family in breakfast prep. Plus, it allows everyone to customize their burrito exactly how they like it. You can even have theme days where you try out different combinations and vote on your favorites. It's a fun, interactive way to enjoy breakfast together.

Breakfast burritos are not just a meal; they're a canvas for your culinary creativity. They're quick, easy, and versatile, making them the perfect breakfast for busy mornings. So, grab your tortillas, pick your favorite fillings, and start wrapping. You'll have a delicious, portable breakfast ready in no time, and you might even discover some new favorite flavor combinations along the way.

FUN AND FRUITY PARFAITS

Imagine starting your day with a breakfast that looks like a rainbow in a glass. Parfaits are a fun and healthy way to kick off your morning. They're all about layers – creamy yogurt, sweet fruit, and crunchy granola. Each spoonful is a delightful mix of textures and flavors. Plus, they're super easy to make and customize, making them perfect for kids and teens who want a quick but delicious breakfast.

Let's begin with a basic parfait recipe. You'll need yogurt, fresh fruit, and granola. Grab a glass or a jar and start with a layer of yogurt at the bottom. Next, add a layer of fresh fruit. You can use anything you like – strawberries, blueberries, kiwi, or even a mix. Then, sprinkle a layer of granola on top. Repeat these layers until you fill the glass or jar. The result is a beautiful, colorful parfait that's as fun to look at as it is to eat. The best part? You can make these parfaits the night before and grab them on your way out the door in the morning.

To make your parfaits even more interesting and visually appealing, try using different fruits for each layer. For example, start with strawberries for the first layer, then add blueberries for the next, and finish with kiwi on top. This creates a vibrant, colorful effect that makes your parfait look like a work of art. You can also add a drizzle of honey or a dollop of nut butter between the layers for an extra burst of flavor. Imagine a parfait with creamy yogurt, juicy fruit, crunchy granola, and a swirl of almond butter – it's like having dessert for breakfast, but much healthier.

Now, let's explore some delicious parfait variations. The Tropical Parfait is perfect for those who love a taste of the tropics. Use coconut yogurt as your base, and layer it with pineapple chunks, mango slices, and toasted coconut flakes. Each spoonful will transport you to a sunny beach. If you're a chocolate lover, the Chocolate Lovers Parfait is for you. Start with chocolate yogurt, then add banana slices and chocolate chips. It's a decadent treat that feels indulgent but is still healthy. For a berry-packed breakfast, try the Berry Blast

Parfait. Use mixed berry yogurt, fresh berries, and a spoonful of berry compote for a burst of fruity goodness in every bite.

Parfaits are not just about taste; they're also about presentation. When layering your ingredients, think about creating a visually appealing pattern. Use different colors and textures to make each layer stand out. For example, place bright red strawberries next to dark blue blueberries, and add a layer of crunchy granola in between. This not only makes your parfait look beautiful but also ensures that each bite is full of different flavors and textures. You can even try making shapes or letters with your fruit slices for a fun twist.

Here's a little tip: if you're making parfaits for a group, set up a parfait bar. Lay out bowls of yogurt, various fruits, and granola, and let everyone build their own parfait. This is a great way to involve your friends or family in breakfast prep and allows everyone to customize their parfaits to their liking. Plus, it's a fun and interactive way to start the day together.

Parfaits are a fantastic way to enjoy a healthy, balanced breakfast that's quick and easy to make. They're perfect for busy mornings or as a special treat on the weekends. With endless possibilities for customization, you can experiment with different flavors and ingredients to find your perfect combination. So, grab your yogurt, fruit, and granola, and start layering. You'll have a delicious, nutritious breakfast ready in no time, and you might even discover some new favorite flavors along the way.

Breakfast is the most important meal of the day, and with these fun and easy recipes, you'll be excited to get up and start cooking. From smoothie bowls and overnight oats to pancakes and burritos, there's something for everyone. These recipes not only taste great but also give you the energy and nutrients you need to tackle whatever the day throws at you. Now, let's move on to the next chapter, where we'll explore even more delicious and easy-to-make meals.

CHAPTER 3

Snack Attack

Hey there, snack lovers! Picture this: it's a lazy afternoon, and you're feeling a bit hungry. You want something tasty, but you also want it to be healthy and satisfying. Enter the world of snacks that are both fun to eat and good for you. Today, we're diving into the realm of veggie sticks and dips. Trust me, crunchy veggie sticks can turn a boring snack time into a colorful, delicious adventure. Plus, they're packed with vitamins and fiber to keep you fueled and happy.

QUICK AND CRUNCHY VEGGIE STICKS WITH DIPS

Veggie sticks are a fantastic snack option for many reasons. First off, they're incredibly healthy. Vegetables are packed with essential vitamins and fiber, which are crucial for your growth and well-being. Eating a variety of colorful veggies ensures you get a range of nutrients. For example, carrots are high in vitamin A, which is great for your eyesight, while bell peppers are rich in vitamin C, boosting your immune system. Plus, the fiber in veggies helps keep you full and satisfied, making them a great choice for curbing those afternoon munchies without reaching for something sugary or processed.

Now, let's talk about some kid-friendly veggies that are easy to prepare and super appealing. Carrot sticks are a classic. They're sweet, crunchy, and easy to cut into perfect dipping sticks. Cucumber slices are another hit, with their refreshing crunch that's perfect for a hot day. Bell pepper strips come in vibrant colors like red, yellow, and orange, making your snack plate look like a rainbow. Cherry tomatoes are little bursts of juicy goodness that are fun to pop into your mouth. Snap peas offer a satisfying snap and a touch of sweetness, and celery sticks are perfect for scooping up thick dips. These veggies aren't just tasty; they're also visually appealing, which makes snack time more exciting.

But what's a crunchy veggie without a delicious dip? Let's whip up some simple and tasty dip recipes that pair perfectly with your veggie sticks. First up, we have a classic hummus. Made from blended chickpeas, tahini, lemon juice, and garlic, hummus is creamy, nutritious, and incredibly easy to make. Just toss all the ingredients into a food processor, blend until smooth, and you're good to go. Next, we have a ranch dip made with Greek yogurt. Mix Greek yogurt with a bit of garlic powder, onion powder, dried dill, and a pinch of salt. This dip is creamy and tangy, with a fraction of the calories of traditional ranch dressing. Lastly, let's not forget guacamole. Mash up some ripe avocados with lime juice, a sprinkle of salt, and a bit of diced tomato and onion if you like. Guacamole is rich, creamy, and packed with heart-healthy fats.

Presentation is key when it comes to making veggie sticks and dips look as appealing as they taste. Start by arranging your veggies in colorful patterns on a large platter. You can make a rainbow with bell pepper strips, cucumber slices, and carrot sticks, or create fun shapes like a sunburst with cherry tomatoes in the center. Use small, fun bowls for your dips to add a touch of whimsy to your snack spread. You can even label the dips with cute tags to make it feel like a mini buffet. A beautifully arranged veggie platter not only looks inviting but also makes you more excited to eat your veggies.

Here's a little tip to make your veggie sticks even more fun to eat: try cutting them into different shapes. Use a crinkle cutter for a wavy effect on your cucumber slices or carrot sticks. You can also use small cookie cutters to create fun shapes out of bell pepper strips or cucumber rounds. This adds an element of surprise and makes your snack time even more enjoyable. Plus, it's a great way to get creative in the kitchen and make your snacks look as good as they taste.

Veggie sticks and dips are not just a snack; they're a celebration of flavors, colors, and textures. They're a healthy, tasty, and satisfying option for any time of the day. So, grab your favorite veggies, whip up some delicious dips, and get ready to crunch your way to a healthier you. Enjoy every bite and have fun experimenting with different veggies and dip combinations!

DIY TRAIL MIX: MIX AND MATCH

Ever find yourself craving a snack that's both tasty and portable? Trail mix is your answer. It's the ultimate on-the-go snack, perfect for tossing in your backpack before heading to school or munching on during a study break. The best part about making your own trail mix is the endless possibilities. You can personalize it with your favorite ingredients, ensuring each handful is just the way you like it. Whether you're a fan of sweet, salty, or a mix of both, trail mix has got you covered.

Creating your own trail mix starts with a few basic components. Nuts and seeds form the backbone of any good mix. Almonds, cashews, and sunflower seeds are all excellent choices. They provide a satisfying crunch and are packed with protein and healthy fats to keep you energized. Then come the dried fruits. Raisins are a classic, but don't stop there. Try adding dried cranberries for a tart twist or dried apricots for a bit of sweetness. These fruits are not only delicious but also add a chewy texture that contrasts nicely with the crunch of the nuts.

Now, let's talk about the fun extras that take your trail mix to the next level. Chocolate chips are always a hit, adding a bit of indulgence to each bite. Pretzels bring a salty crunch that balances out the sweetness of the dried fruits and chocolate. For something a bit different, try adding popcorn. It's light, airy, and adds another layer of texture. You can even throw in some mini marshmallows or M&Ms for a colorful and fun addition. The beauty of trail mix is that you can mix and match these components to create a snack that's uniquely yours.

Let's explore some flavor combinations to get you started. For a classic sweet and salty mix, combine pretzels, peanuts, and chocolate chips. The saltiness of the pretzels and peanuts pairs perfectly with the sweetness of the chocolate. If you're in the mood for something tropical, try a mix of dried pineapple, coconut flakes, and macadamia nuts. It's like a mini vacation in every bite. For those who love the classics, a simple mix of raisins, peanuts, and M&Ms never fails. It's a nostalgic combination that's sure to hit the spot every time.

Storing your trail mix properly is key to keeping it fresh and crunchy. Use airtight containers or zip-lock bags to store your mix. These keep out moisture and air, which can make your ingredients go stale. If you're planning to take your trail mix on the go, pre-portion it into snack-sized bags. This not only makes it convenient to grab and go but also helps with portion control. You can easily pop a bag into your lunchbox or gym bag, ensuring you always have a healthy snack on hand.

Here's a pro tip: get creative with your trail mix by adding seasonal ingredients. For example, during the fall, try adding some pumpkin seeds and dried cranberries for a festive twist. In the summer, dried mango and coconut flakes can give your mix a tropical vibe. You can also experiment with different spices. A sprinkle of cinnamon can add warmth and depth to your mix, while a touch of sea salt can enhance the flavors of the nuts and chocolate. The possibilities are endless, and part of the fun is experimenting to find your perfect combination.

Making your own trail mix is not just about having a tasty snack; it's also about the joy of creating something that's uniquely yours. It's a fun and easy way to explore different flavors and textures, and it's a snack that can adapt to your changing tastes and preferences. So grab your ingredients, mix and match to your heart's content, and enjoy the delicious results.

CHEESE AND FRUIT KABOBS

Imagine having a snack that's not only delicious but also looks like a mini piece of art. Cheese and fruit kabobs are exactly that—fun to make, nutritious, and visually appealing. They combine protein from the cheese and vitamins from the fruit, creating a balanced snack that keeps you energized and satisfied. Plus, they're super easy to put together, making them a perfect choice for kids and teens looking to whip up something tasty in no time.

Let's start with some classic cheese and fruit combinations that work well together. Cheddar and apple are a match made in heaven. The sharpness of the cheddar pairs beautifully with the sweet, crisp apple slices. Mozzarella and grape are another fantastic duo. The mild, creamy mozzarella complements the juicy burst of flavor from the grapes. Gouda and pear, on the other hand, offer a slightly more sophisticated taste. The buttery gouda melds perfectly with the sweet, smooth texture of the pear. These combinations not only taste great but also provide a variety of textures and flavors in each bite.

Now, let's get down to assembling these kabobs. First, gather your ingredients: blocks of cheese and fresh fruit. Start by cutting the cheese and fruit into bite-sized pieces. Aim for uniform sizes so that they look neat and are easy to eat. Once you have your pieces ready, grab some skewers or colorful toothpicks. Begin by skewer a piece of cheese, followed by a piece of fruit, and repeat. Mixing up the order adds visual appeal and ensures a delightful mix of flavors in every bite. Continue until you've used up your ingredients or filled your skewers. It's a simple process, but the result is a snack that looks as good as it tastes.

Creative presentation can make your cheese and fruit kabobs even more appealing. Arrange them on a platter in a starburst pattern, with the skewers radiating out from the center like the rays of the sun. This not only looks inviting but also makes it easy for everyone to grab a kabob. Using colorful skewers or toothpicks adds an extra touch of fun. You can find them in various shapes and colors, making your snack even more festive. Imagine a platter full of bright, colorful kabobs at your next family gathering or picnic. It's sure to be a hit!

Here's a little tip to make your kabobs even more exciting: try adding a drizzle of honey or a sprinkle of cinnamon on the fruit before assembling. This adds an extra layer of flavor and makes your kabobs feel like a special treat. You can also experiment with different types of cheese and fruit combinations. For example, try using brie with apple slices for a creamy, luxurious taste, or pair sharp provolone with strawberries for a bold flavor contrast. The possibilities are endless, and part of the fun is discovering new combinations that you love.

Cheese and fruit kabobs are not just a snack; they're a fun and creative way to enjoy healthy foods. They're quick to make, easy to customize, and perfect for any occasion. Whether you're looking for a quick after-school snack or a fun addition to a party spread, these kabobs are a great choice. So, grab your cheese, pick your favorite fruits, and start assembling. You'll have a delicious, nutritious snack ready in no time, and you might even discover some new favorite flavor combinations along the way.

NO-BAKE ENERGY BITES

Imagine you're in the middle of a busy afternoon, maybe working on homework or getting ready for sports practice, and you need a quick snack to keep you going. No-bake energy bites are perfect for these moments. They're packed with nutrients, super easy to make, and give you that much-needed energy boost. Think of them as little power balls that you can whip up in no time and take with you anywhere. They're made from ingredients that provide a good mix of protein, healthy fats, and carbs, which help keep your energy levels steady and your hunger at bay.

Let's start with a basic recipe that you can follow easily. You'll need a few simple ingredients: oats, honey, peanut butter, and chocolate chips. First, grab a mixing bowl and add one cup of rolled oats. Next, pour in half a cup of peanut butter. If your peanut butter is a bit thick, you can microwave it for a few seconds to make it easier to mix. Now, add one-third cup of honey. This not only helps to bind everything together but also adds natural sweetness. Finally, toss in half a cup of chocolate chips. Mix everything until well combined. Once your mixture is ready, scoop out small portions and roll them into balls. Place the balls on a baking sheet and pop them in the refrigerator for about an hour to set. That's it! You've got yourself a batch of delicious energy bites.

To keep things interesting, you can experiment with different flavor variations. For a tropical twist, try adding shredded coconut and chocolate chips to your mixture. The coconut adds a chewy texture and pairs perfectly with the chocolate. If you're a fan of tart flavors, mix in some dried cranberries and chopped almonds. The cranberries add a burst of tangy sweetness, while the almonds provide a satisfying crunch. For those who love a classic combination, try adding mashed banana and chopped walnuts. The banana adds moisture and a natural sweetness, while the walnuts give a rich, nutty flavor. Each variation brings a unique taste and texture, making your energy bites even more enjoyable.

Storing your energy bites properly is key to keeping them fresh and delicious. Once your bites are set, transfer them to an airtight container. This helps keep out moisture and air, which can make them go stale. Store the container in the refrigerator, where the bites will stay fresh for up to a week. If you want to make a larger batch and save some for later, you can also freeze them. Just place the bites on a baking sheet and freeze them for an hour. Once they're frozen, transfer them to a zip-lock bag or freezer-safe container. They'll keep in the freezer for up to a month. When you're ready to eat, just grab a bite or two and let them thaw for a few minutes.

Here's a handy tip: if you're making energy bites for a group, set up a DIY energy bite bar. Lay out all the basic ingredients and a variety of add-ins like dried fruits, nuts, and seeds. Let everyone mix and match their own combinations. This not only makes the process more fun but also allows everyone to create their perfect snack. Plus, it's a great way to involve friends or family in the kitchen and share the joy of making something delicious together.

No-bake energy bites are not just a snack; they're a quick and easy way to fuel your body with wholesome ingredients. They're perfect for busy days when you need a boost or as a treat to enjoy anytime. So, gather your ingredients, mix up a batch, and enjoy the delicious, nutritious benefits of these little power balls. Each bite is a reminder that healthy snacks can be fun, tasty, and incredibly satisfying.

POPCORN PARTY MIX

Imagine hosting a movie night with friends or family and needing the perfect snack to match the fun. Popcorn party mixes are the ultimate solution. They combine different flavors and textures, creating a snack that everyone will love. Whether you like sweet, salty, savory, or a bit of spice, there's a popcorn mix variation for you. Plus, they're great for sharing and perfect for parties, making snack time a festive event.

Let's start with a basic popcorn mix recipe that's easy to put together. You'll need some popped popcorn, pretzels, M&Ms, and nuts. Begin by popping a big bowl of popcorn. You can use microwave popcorn or pop your own on the stove. Next, grab a large mixing bowl and add the popped popcorn. Toss in a handful of pretzels for some salty crunch. Add a generous amount of M&Ms for a pop of color and sweetness. Finally, throw in some nuts like almonds or peanuts for an extra layer of flavor and texture. Mix everything well, and there you have it—a delicious, fun popcorn party mix ready to enjoy.

But why stop at the basics? Let's explore some exciting flavor variations to cater to different tastes. For those who love the classic sweet and salty combo, try mixing caramel popcorn with pretzels and chocolate chips. The caramel adds a rich, buttery sweetness that pairs perfectly with the salty pretzels and creamy chocolate. If you're in the mood for something savory, combine cheddar popcorn with nuts and cheese crackers. The cheddar popcorn brings a sharp, tangy flavor, while the nuts and crackers add crunch and depth. For those who enjoy a bit of heat, try a spicy mix with spicy popcorn, tortilla chips, and roasted chickpeas. The tortilla chips add a nice crunch, and the roasted chickpeas bring a smoky, spicy kick that keeps you coming back for more.

Presentation is key when serving your popcorn party mix. Use colorful bowls or bags to make your snack spread look inviting and festive. You can create individual snack-sized portions by filling small paper bags or cups with the mix. This makes it easy for everyone to grab their own portion and enjoy without having to share from a communal bowl. For a fun touch, label each bowl or bag with the flavor variation, so everyone knows what they're getting. You can even add a little flair with decorative labels or tags.

Here's a pro tip: if you're making popcorn party mix for a larger group, consider setting up a popcorn bar. Lay out different types of popcorn, like plain, caramel, and cheddar, along with a variety of mix-ins like pretzels, nuts, and candy. Let everyone create their own customized mix. This not only makes the process interactive and fun but also ensures that everyone gets a snack they love. Plus, it's a great conversation starter and adds an element of excitement to your event.

Popcorn party mixes are not just about flavor; they're also about fun and creativity. They're a versatile snack that you can easily adapt to your preferences and the occasion. Whether you're hosting a movie night, a birthday party, or just looking for a fun snack to share with friends, popcorn party mixes are the way to go. So grab your ingredients, get mixing, and enjoy the delightful combination of flavors and textures that make popcorn party mixes a hit.

CHAPTER 4

Lunchbox Heroes

Picture this: It's a busy school day, and lunchtime rolls around. You open your lunchbox, and there it is—a boring, soggy sandwich. Not exactly thrilling, right? Now imagine instead pulling out a delicious, neatly wrapped sandwich wrap that's packed with all your favorite flavors. Suddenly, lunchtime just got a whole lot more exciting. That's the magic of sandwich wraps. They're not only portable and less messy than traditional sandwiches, but they're also super versatile. You can customize them with endless combinations of fillings, making each lunch unique and exciting.

WRAP IT UP: EASY SANDWICH WRAPS

Sandwich wraps are a fantastic lunch option for several reasons. First, they're easy to make. You can throw together a wrap in just a few minutes, which is perfect for those hectic mornings when you're rushing out the door. Plus, they're portable and less messy than traditional sandwiches. The tortilla keeps everything neatly contained, so you don't have to worry about fillings falling out or the bread getting soggy. This makes them perfect for packing in your lunchbox, whether you're heading to school, practice, or a day out.

Assembling a basic wrap is super simple. Start with a soft tortilla—whole wheat or regular flour tortillas work best. Lay the tortilla flat on a clean surface. Next, choose your protein. This could be slices of turkey, chicken, or even a plant-based option like hummus. Spread the protein evenly over the tortilla. Now, add your veggies. Think lettuce, tomatoes, cucumber slices, or bell peppers. These add a nice crunch and lots of vitamins. To make your wrap even tastier, add a spread like hummus, mayo, or mustard. Spread it evenly over the tortilla to help hold everything together. Finally, roll the tortilla tightly from one end to the other. If needed, secure the wrap with toothpicks to keep it from unrolling. Cut the wrap in half for easier handling, and you're good to go!

But why stop at the basics? Let's explore some creative wrap ideas that will keep your lunches interesting. How about a Mediterranean Wrap? Start with a layer of hummus, then add grilled chicken, cucumber slices, feta cheese, and a few olives. The combination of creamy hummus and tangy feta is simply irresistible. If you're looking for something lighter, try a Veggie Delight wrap. Spread some avocado on the tortilla, then layer on spinach, bell peppers, shredded carrots, and a bit of hummus. This wrap is not only colorful but also packed with nutrients. For those who love a bit of BBQ flavor, the BBQ Chicken Wrap is a must-try. Spread some BBQ sauce on the tortilla, add shredded chicken, a scoop of coleslaw, and a sprinkle of cheddar cheese. The result is a wrap that's bursting with flavor in every bite.

Keeping your wraps fresh until lunchtime is key to enjoying them at their best. Start by wrapping them tightly in foil or parchment paper. This helps to hold everything together and prevents the wrap from getting soggy. If you're packing the wrap in a lunchbox, use a lunchbox with an ice pack to keep the ingredients cool and fresh. This is especially important if your wrap contains perishable items like meat or cheese. Another tip is to keep any wet ingredients, like tomatoes or pickles, separate and add them just before eating. This helps to keep the tortilla from getting soggy and ensures your wrap stays crisp and delicious.

With these tips and ideas, you're all set to become a lunchbox hero. Sandwich wraps are not just a quick and easy lunch option; they're also a canvas for your culinary creativity. You can mix and match ingredients to create endless combinations, ensuring your lunch is always exciting and never boring. So, grab your ingredients, roll up a delicious wrap, and enjoy a lunch that's as fun to make as it is to eat.

BENTO BOX FUN: BALANCED MEAL IDEAS

Imagine opening your lunchbox and finding a colorful, perfectly organized meal that looks as good as it tastes. That's the beauty of bento boxes. These compartmentalized containers are like little treasure chests for your food, keeping everything neat and separated. Bento boxes are ideal for balanced lunches because they encourage you to include a variety of foods—proteins, carbs, and veggies—all in one convenient package. Plus, they're super fun to put together and can make lunchtime something you look forward to.

So, what exactly should you put in your bento box to make it balanced and delicious? Start with a main protein. This could be grilled chicken, tofu, or even hard-boiled eggs. Proteins are essential for keeping you full and giving you the energy you need to get through the day. Next, add some carbs. Rice, pasta, or a slice of bread are great options that provide the fuel your body needs. Then, don't forget the veggies. Sliced cucumbers, cherry tomatoes, and carrot sticks add a crunch and a burst of color to your meal. Finally, throw in some extras like fruit slices, cheese cubes, or a handful of nuts to round out your lunch.

Let's get creative with some fun bento box combinations. How about a Sushi Bento? Start with cucumber sushi rolls, which are not only tasty but also easy to make. Add some edamame for protein and a side of orange slices for a refreshing finish. Not only is this bento box visually appealing, but it also offers a great balance of flavors and textures. If you're in the mood for something a bit more classic, try a Picnic Bento. This one features mini sandwiches, grapes, baby carrots, and cheese sticks. It's like having a mini picnic right in your lunchbox. For a bit of a twist, the Taco Bento is a hit. Pack tortillas, beans, cheese, and salsa in separate compartments, so you can build your own tacos at lunchtime. Each bite is a new adventure, and you get to enjoy the fun of assembling your meal.

Packing your bento box properly is key to keeping everything fresh and organized. One trick is to use silicone cups to separate different foods. This not only keeps your ingredients from mixing but also adds a pop of color to your box. For example, you can use a silicone cup to hold your cherry tomatoes or cheese cubes. It makes everything look neat and makes it easier to eat. Another tip is to pack wet items separately to avoid sogginess. For example, if you're including a dip or sauce, put it in a small, sealed container to keep it from spilling onto your other foods. Finally, make sure your bento box is properly sealed. A good seal keeps everything in place and prevents leaks, which means your lunch stays fresh and intact until you're ready to eat.

Bento boxes are not just about packing food; they're about making your meal visually appealing and balanced. Each compartment offers a different taste and texture, making lunchtime exciting. Whether you're packing a lunch for school, a day out, or even just for fun at home, bento boxes are a fantastic option. They encourage you to eat a balanced meal and make the whole process of packing and eating lunch enjoyable. So, next time you're wondering what to pack for lunch, think bento. Grab your favorite ingredients, get creative with the combinations, and enjoy a delicious, balanced meal that's as fun to make as it is to eat.

ALLERGY-FRIENDLY LUNCHES

Imagine being at school and opening your lunchbox only to find foods you can't eat because of allergies. It's not just disappointing; it can be dangerous. That's why having allergy-friendly lunch options is so important. These options ensure that kids with dietary restrictions can enjoy their meals safely and comfortably. Making sure everyone can participate in lunchtime without worry promotes inclusivity and awareness. Whether it's dairy, nuts, or gluten, there are plenty of tasty alternatives available.

Let's start by identifying some of the most common allergens and their suitable substitutions. If you're allergic to dairy, you can easily swap out regular milk with plant-based options like almond milk, soy milk, or oat milk. Vegan cheese comes in various flavors and textures, making it a great substitute for traditional cheese. For those with nut allergies, sunflower seeds and sunflower butter are excellent alternatives. They provide a similar texture and taste without the risk. Gluten can be tricky, but don't worry—there are plenty of gluten-free options out there. You can use gluten-free bread, wraps, and pasta to make sure your meals are safe and delicious.

Now, let's get creative with some allergy-friendly lunch ideas. How about a Dairy-Free Pizza? Start with a dairy-free crust and spread a generous layer of marinara sauce. Top it with vegan cheese and your favorite veggies. Bake until the cheese is melted and bubbly. This pizza is so tasty, you won't even miss the dairy. For a classic favorite, try a Nut-Free PB&J. Use sunflower butter in place of peanut butter and pair it with seedless jam. Spread it on gluten-free bread for an extra allergy-friendly twist. Another great option is a Gluten-Free Pasta Salad. Cook your favorite gluten-free pasta and toss it with a mix of colorful veggies like bell peppers, cherry tomatoes, and cucumbers. Add a light vinaigrette dressing, and you've got a refreshing, nutritious lunch.

Preventing cross-contamination is crucial when preparing and packing allergy-friendly lunches. Always use separate utensils and cutting boards for allergen-containing foods. This helps to avoid any accidental mixing of allergens. Make sure to wash your hands and surfaces thoroughly before and after handling different ingredients. Cleanliness is key to keeping everyone safe. Another helpful tip is to clearly label allergen-free items. This ensures that there's no confusion about what's safe to eat. A simple label or sticker on the container can make a big difference.

Here's a practical tip for you: if you're packing a lunch for someone with severe allergies, consider creating a checklist of safe foods and possible cross-contamination risks. This can help you stay organized and ensure that you're covering all the bases. For example, if you're making a Nut-Free PB&J, your checklist might include checking the bread for nut traces, washing the knife thoroughly, and labeling the sandwich bag as nut-free.

Another fun idea is to get creative with your lunch presentation. Use colorful containers and fun labels to make allergy-friendly lunches look as appealing as possible. Bento boxes with separate compartments are perfect for this. They keep each item separate and prevent any accidental mixing. Plus, they make your lunch look neat and organized, which is always a plus.

Allergy-friendly lunches don't have to be boring or complicated. With a bit of creativity and the right substitutions, you can enjoy a variety of tasty and safe meals. Whether it's a dairy-free pizza, a nut-free PB&J, or a gluten-free pasta salad, there's something for everyone. So, grab your ingredients, follow these tips, and enjoy a delicious and worry-free lunch.

SUPER SIMPLE SOUPS

Imagine coming home after a long day at school, and the comforting aroma of soup fills the kitchen. Soups are one of the most comforting lunch options you can have. They're warm, soothing, and packed with nutrients to keep you energized throughout the day. The best part? You can prepare them in advance and reheat them whenever you want a quick, nutritious meal. Whether it's a chilly day or you just need something warm and cozy, soups are a perfect choice. Plus, they're loaded with vegetables and other healthy ingredients that provide essential vitamins and minerals.

Making soup is easier than you might think. The basic technique starts with sautéing some veggies. Grab a large pot and add a bit of oil. Once the oil is hot, toss in chopped onions, carrots, and celery. These veggies form the base of many soups and add a ton of flavor. Sauté them until they're soft and fragrant. Next, add your broth. You can use chicken, vegetable, or beef broth, depending on your preference. Now it's time to add your protein. This could be shredded chicken, beans, or even tofu. Let everything simmer together until the flavors meld and the ingredients are cooked through. Simmering allows the flavors to deepen and the ingredients to become tender.

Let's dive into some simple soup recipes that you can easily make at home. Chicken Noodle Soup is a classic favorite. Start with a base of sautéed carrots, celery, and onions. Add chicken broth and bring it to a boil. Toss in shredded cooked chicken and egg noodles. Let it simmer until the noodles are tender. This soup is not only delicious but also incredibly comforting. Another great option is Tomato Basil Soup. Use fresh tomatoes if you can, and add them to a pot with sautéed onions and garlic. Pour in some vegetable broth and let it simmer. Blend the soup until smooth, then stir in fresh basil for a burst of flavor. For a hearty, vegetarian option, try Veggie Lentil Soup. Sauté onions, carrots, and garlic in a pot. Add in lentils, vegetable broth, and a handful of spinach. Let it simmer until the lentils are tender. This soup is packed with nutrients and is incredibly satisfying.

Packing and reheating soup for lunch requires a bit of planning but is totally worth it. If you want to keep your soup hot until lunchtime, use a thermos. Preheat the thermos by filling it with hot water for a few minutes, then pour out the water and add your hot soup. This helps to keep the soup warm for hours. If you prefer to reheat your soup at school, pack it in a microwave-safe container. When it's time to eat, simply pop it in the microwave for a minute or two. Don't forget to bring a spoon and a napkin for convenience. A small, foldable spoon can easily fit into your lunchbox and makes eating soup a breeze.

Here's a handy tip: if you're packing soup with lots of ingredients like noodles or beans, give it a good stir before reheating to ensure everything heats evenly. Also, consider packing a small piece of bread or some crackers to go along with your soup. They add a nice crunch and make your meal even more enjoyable.

Another way to elevate your soup experience is by adding garnishes. Fresh herbs like parsley or cilantro, a sprinkle of grated cheese, or a dollop of sour cream can take your soup to the next level. These little touches not only add extra flavor but also make your meal look more appealing. Imagine opening your thermos to find a fragrant, steamy soup with a sprinkle of fresh herbs on top. It's a small detail that makes a big difference.

Soups are a fantastic way to enjoy a healthy, balanced lunch that's both delicious and easy to prepare. With these simple techniques and recipes, you'll be able to whip up a variety of soups that will keep you warm, satisfied, and ready to take on the day. So grab your ingredients, get cooking, and enjoy the comforting goodness of homemade soup.

COLORFUL PASTA SALADS

Imagine opening your lunchbox to find a vibrant, colorful pasta salad that's both delicious and nutritious. Pasta salads are a fantastic lunch option because they can be served cold or at room temperature, making them perfect for school or a day out. They're incredibly versatile, allowing you to customize them with your favorite ingredients. Plus, they're easy to make and store, giving you a hearty lunch that's ready whenever you are.

Let's start with a basic pasta salad recipe. You'll need some cooked pasta, a selection of fresh veggies, and a tasty dressing. Begin by cooking your pasta according to the package instructions. Once cooked, drain and rinse it under cold water to stop the cooking process and cool it down. In a large bowl, combine the pasta with chopped bell peppers, cherry tomatoes, and any other veggies you like. For the dressing, a simple Italian or vinaigrette works wonders. Pour the dressing over the pasta and veggies, then toss everything together until well coated. There you have it—a simple, delicious pasta salad that's ready to enjoy.

But why stop at basic? Let's explore some creative pasta salad ideas that will keep your lunches exciting. How about a Greek Pasta Salad? Combine cooked pasta with olives, crumbled feta cheese, sliced cucumber, and thinly sliced red onion. Toss with a lemony vinaigrette for a burst of Mediterranean flavor. If you're a fan of fresh, classic flavors, a Caprese Pasta Salad is a must-try. Mix pasta with fresh mozzarella balls, cherry tomatoes, and basil leaves. Drizzle with a balsamic glaze and a bit of olive oil for a salad that's as beautiful as it is tasty. For those who love a rainbow on their plate, a Veggie Rainbow Pasta Salad is perfect. Use a variety of colorful vegetables like carrots, bell peppers, purple cabbage, and peas. Toss with a light vinaigrette, and you've got a feast for the eyes and the stomach.

Packing and serving your pasta salad properly is key to keeping it fresh and delicious. Use airtight containers to store your pasta salad. This helps to keep the flavors locked in and prevents the salad from drying out. If you're not eating the salad right away, keep the dressing separate until you're ready to eat. This prevents the pasta from getting soggy. When it's time for lunch, simply pour the dressing over the salad and give it a good toss. Don't forget to pack a fork and napkin for convenience. A small container or a zip-lock bag for the dressing can make it easy to add right before eating.

Here's a handy tip: if you're making pasta salad in advance, consider using sturdier pasta shapes like rotini or penne. These shapes hold up well in the fridge and maintain their texture better than more delicate pastas. You can also add a bit of extra dressing just before serving to freshen up the flavors. Adding fresh herbs like parsley or cilantro right before eating can also elevate the taste and make your salad even more enjoyable.

Pasta salads are not just a lunch; they're a delightful medley of flavors and textures that can make your midday meal something to look forward to. They're easy to customize, simple to pack, and delicious to eat. Whether you stick to a basic recipe or get creative with different ingredients, pasta salads are a versatile and colorful option that's sure to satisfy. So grab your favorite ingredients, mix up a delicious pasta salad, and enjoy a lunch that's both fun to make and delightful to eat.

Lunch should never be boring, and with these tasty and creative ideas, yours never will be. Whether you're rolling up a wrap, packing a bento box, making an allergy-friendly meal, or enjoying a warm soup or a vibrant pasta salad, you're all set to become a true lunchbox hero. Ready for more? Let's move on to exploring some exciting after-school munchies that are just as fun and delicious.

CHAPTER 5

After-School Munchies

Imagine this: You've just finished a long day at school, and you walk into the kitchen with a rumbling stomach. You need something quick, delicious, and fun to make. Enter after-school munchies—the snacks that are not only easy to whip up but also super tasty and customizable. These snacks are designed to keep you fueled and happy until dinner time, and the best part? You can get creative with them. Let's kick things off with a snack that everyone loves—mini pizzas.

DIY MINI PIZZAS

Mini pizzas are the ultimate after-school snack. They're fun to make, easy to customize, and they allow you to get creative with your favorite toppings. Imagine having your own personal pizza, hot and bubbly, ready in just a few minutes. That's the magic of mini pizzas. They're perfect for when you want something quick but satisfying, and the best part is that you can make them exactly how you like.

To start, let's go over the basic ingredients you'll need for mini pizzas: English muffins or small pita bread, tomato sauce, and shredded cheese. These ingredients are simple and likely already in your pantry or fridge. Begin by preheating your oven to 375°F (190°C). While the oven heats up, split the English muffins or pita bread in half and place them on a baking sheet lined with parchment paper. This will prevent them from sticking and make cleanup a breeze. Spread a spoonful of tomato sauce on each half, making sure to cover the entire surface. Next, sprinkle a generous amount of shredded cheese over the sauce. Now, they're ready to bake! Pop the baking sheet in the oven and bake for about 10 minutes or until the cheese is melted and bubbly.

But why stop at basic cheese pizzas? The real fun comes in when you start adding your favorite toppings. If you're a fan of classic flavors, try adding slices of pepperoni, mushrooms, and bell peppers. For a taste of the tropics, add some pineapple chunks, ham, and olives. If you're in the mood for something a bit more gourmet, try a combination of spinach, feta cheese, and sun-dried tomatoes. The possibilities are endless, and you can mix and match toppings to create your perfect mini pizza. Each bite is a burst of flavor, and you get to experiment with different combinations.

Here are some tips to make sure your mini pizzas turn out perfectly every time. First, make sure to preheat your oven to the right temperature. This ensures that the pizzas cook evenly and the cheese melts beautifully. Using a baking sheet lined with parchment paper not only prevents sticking but also makes it easy to transfer the pizzas to a plate. When it comes to baking, keep an eye on the pizzas. You want the cheese to be golden and bubbly, indicating that it's perfectly melted. If you like your crust a bit crispier, you can leave them in for an extra minute or two, but be careful not to overcook them.

Here's a fun idea: set up a mini pizza bar. Lay out all the ingredients and let your friends or family build their own mini pizzas. It's a great way to get everyone involved and allows each person to customize their pizza just how they like it. You can even have themed pizza nights where you try out different combinations and vote on your favorites. It's not just about making a snack; it's about creating a fun and interactive experience in the kitchen.

Mini pizzas are a fantastic way to enjoy a delicious, personalized snack that's quick and easy to make. They're perfect for after-school munchies, and the customization options are endless. So, grab your ingredients, get creative with your toppings, and enjoy a tasty mini pizza that's made just for you.

LOADED NACHOS

Picture this: you're hanging out after school, and a wave of hunger hits. What could be more satisfying than a plate of loaded nachos? Nachos are the perfect snack because they combine crunchy, cheesy, and savory elements all in one bite. They're easy to share with friends and family, making them ideal for any gathering or a quick solo snack. The best part? You can customize them with all your favorite toppings, making each plate uniquely delicious.

To get started, let's talk about the basic ingredients you'll need for loaded nachos: tortilla chips, shredded cheese, black beans, and salsa. These ingredients are simple and versatile, ensuring you can whip up a tasty snack in no time. Begin by preheating your oven to 375°F (190°C). While the oven heats up, spread a generous layer of tortilla chips on a baking sheet. Make sure the chips are in a single layer to ensure even melting. Next, sprinkle a good amount of shredded cheese over the chips. Add a layer of black beans, followed by spoonfuls of salsa. Now, pop the baking sheet into the oven and bake for about 10 minutes, or until the cheese is melted and bubbly. The result? A warm, gooey, and satisfying plate of nachos ready to devour.

But why stop at just cheese, beans, and salsa? Let's explore some creative topping ideas to make your nachos even more exciting. If you love a bit of protein, try adding some ground beef. Cook the beef with a bit of taco seasoning for extra flavor, then sprinkle it over the chips before baking. If you like a bit of heat, add slices of jalapeños. They bring a spicy kick that complements the cheesy goodness. Sour cream is another fantastic addition, adding a cool, creamy contrast to the hot nachos. Guacamole is a must-try topping. Its creamy texture and rich flavor make every bite even more delectable. For a fresh burst of flavor, add diced tomatoes and green onions. They add a pop of color and a crunchy texture that pairs perfectly with the melted cheese. Corn and black olives are also great options, adding sweetness and a slight briny flavor. Finally, top your nachos with shredded lettuce for some extra crunch and freshness.

Once your nachos are loaded with all your favorite toppings, it's time to think about presentation. Serving your nachos on a large platter makes them look inviting and easy to share. Arrange the nachos in a way that showcases the variety of toppings, making each chip look irresistible. You can also serve the nachos with small bowls of dips on the side. Think extra salsa, guacamole, and sour cream. This not only adds variety but also makes it easy for everyone to customize their own nacho experience. A sprinkle of fresh herbs like cilantro or parsley can add a burst of color and a hint of freshness. It's a small touch that makes a big difference in how your nachos look and taste.

Here's a fun idea: make nacho night a regular event. Gather your friends or family, set out all the ingredients, and let everyone build their own plate of nachos. It's a fun and interactive way to enjoy a delicious snack together. You can even have themed nacho nights where you try out different flavor combinations and vote on your favorites. It's not just about the food; it's about creating a fun and memorable experience.

Loaded nachos are more than just a snack; they're a celebration of flavors and textures. They're easy to make, fun to customize, and perfect for any occasion. Whether you're enjoying them alone or sharing with friends, each bite is a delightful mix of crunchy, cheesy, and savory elements that will keep you coming back for more. So, grab your ingredients, get creative with your toppings, and enjoy a plate of loaded nachos that's just as fun to make as it is to eat.

QUICK QUESADILLAS

After school, sometimes you need a snack that's quick, tasty, and easy to make. Quesadillas fit the bill perfectly. These delicious snacks are super versatile and only require a few basic ingredients. Imagine biting into a crispy tortilla filled with gooey, melted cheese and whatever fillings you love most. Whether you're craving something simple or a bit more adventurous, quesadillas can be customized to suit your taste.

To make a basic cheese quesadilla, you'll need tortillas and shredded cheese. Start by heating a skillet over medium heat. Place a tortilla in the skillet and sprinkle an even layer of shredded cheese on top. If you want to add extra fillings, this is the time to do it. Think of ingredients like cooked chicken, black beans, or corn. Once you've added your fillings, top with another tortilla. Cook until the bottom tortilla is golden brown and crispy, then carefully flip the quesadilla with a spatula. Cook the other side until it's also golden and the cheese is fully melted. Remove from the skillet and let it cool slightly before cutting it into wedges.

Now, let's explore some creative filling ideas to keep your quesadillas interesting. If you're a fan of Mexican flavors, try adding cooked chicken, black beans, and corn. The chicken provides protein, while the beans and corn add texture and flavor. For a vegetarian twist, consider filling your quesadilla with spinach, mushrooms, and feta cheese. The spinach and mushrooms are packed with nutrients, and the feta adds a tangy, creamy element. If you're in the mood for something a bit different, how about a ham, pineapple, and mozzarella quesadilla? The combination of savory ham, sweet pineapple, and melty mozzarella is a delightful fusion of flavors that's sure to satisfy your taste buds.

To ensure your quesadillas turn out perfectly crispy and delicious every time, here are a few tips. First, cook them over medium heat. This allows the tortillas to crisp up without burning, while giving the cheese enough time to melt. Use a non-stick skillet or lightly grease your skillet to prevent sticking. When it's time to flip the quesadilla, do so carefully with a spatula to keep all the fillings intact. If you find flipping tricky, you can also make half-moon quesadillas by folding one tortilla in half over the fillings, which makes them easier to handle. Once cooked, let the quesadilla cool for a minute before cutting it into wedges. This helps the cheese set slightly, making it easier to cut and eat.

Here's a fun idea: set up a quesadilla bar where everyone can create their own quesadilla. Lay out a variety of fillings, from meats and beans to veggies and cheeses. Let your friends or family choose their favorite combinations and cook them up on the spot. It's a great way to get everyone involved in the kitchen and allows for endless creativity. You can even have themed nights, like Mexican night with classic fillings or a fusion night with unexpected combinations.

Quesadillas are not just a snack; they're an opportunity to experiment with different flavors and ingredients. They're quick to make, easy to customize, and always satisfying. So, grab some tortillas, choose your favorite fillings, and enjoy a delicious quesadilla that's perfect for any after-school munchies. Each bite is a delightful mix of crispy tortilla and melty cheese, with the added bonus of whatever tasty ingredients you decide to include.

SWEET AND SAVORY POPCORN

Imagine coming home from school and craving a snack that's both fun to eat and easy to make. Popcorn is your perfect go-to. Popcorn is incredibly versatile, making it a fantastic snack for any occasion. You can keep it simple or get creative with different flavors. Whether you're in the mood for something sweet, savory, or even a mix of both, popcorn has got you covered. Plus, it's quick to prepare, so you'll be munching on your tasty treat in no time.

Let's start with a basic stovetop popcorn recipe. You'll need popcorn kernels, oil, and salt. Grab a large pot with a lid and pour in about two tablespoons of oil. You can use coconut oil, vegetable oil, or any high-heat oil you prefer. Heat the oil over medium heat and add a few kernels to test the temperature. Once they pop, you know the oil is ready. Pour in half a cup of popcorn kernels and cover the pot with the lid. Shake the pot gently to make sure the kernels are evenly coated with oil. Keep shaking the pot occasionally to prevent burning and to ensure even popping. Once the popping slows down to a few seconds between pops, remove the pot from the heat. Pour the popcorn into a large bowl and sprinkle with salt to taste. There you have it—light and fluffy popcorn, ready to enjoy.

Now, let's explore the fun part: flavor variations. If you have a sweet tooth, try making caramel popcorn. Melt some butter in a saucepan, add brown sugar and a bit of corn syrup, and let it simmer until it thickens. Pour the caramel over the popcorn and toss until evenly coated. For a simpler sweet option, sprinkle your popcorn with cinnamon sugar. Mix ground cinnamon and sugar, then sprinkle it over the warm popcorn. For chocolate lovers, a chocolate drizzle is a must. Melt some chocolate chips in the microwave and drizzle the melted chocolate over your popcorn. Let it cool for a bit, and you'll have a deliciously sweet treat.

For those who prefer savory snacks, the options are endless. Cheese powder is a classic and easy way to add a burst of flavor. Sprinkle cheese powder over your popcorn while it's still warm so it sticks well. Garlic parmesan popcorn is another favorite. Melt some butter, mix in garlic powder and grated parmesan cheese, and pour it over the popcorn. Toss until the popcorn is evenly coated. If you're in the mood for something with a bit of a kick, try taco seasoning. Mix taco seasoning with a bit of melted butter and drizzle it over the popcorn. Each bite will be a flavorful explosion in your mouth.

Making perfect popcorn every time requires a few tips and tricks. First, using the right oil is crucial. Coconut oil gives a subtle hint of sweetness, while vegetable oil has a neutral flavor. Both work well for popping kernels. To avoid burning the popcorn, keep shaking the pot regularly. This ensures that the kernels heat evenly and pop without burning. Adding flavors while the popcorn is still warm helps them stick better. Whether you're adding salt, cheese powder, or cinnamon sugar, doing it while the popcorn is warm ensures even coating.

Here's a fun idea: set up a popcorn bar for your next movie night. Lay out different toppings and let everyone customize their own popcorn mix. You can have bowls of caramel sauce, cheese powder, chocolate chips, and even mini marshmallows. Not only does this make snack time interactive, but it also allows everyone to create their perfect popcorn blend. Imagine the fun of mixing and matching different flavors and seeing who comes up with the best combination.

Popcorn is more than just a snack; it's a blank canvas for your culinary creativity. It's quick, easy, and endlessly customizable. So, grab your kernels, choose your flavors, and get popping. Each bowl of popcorn is a new adventure in taste, ready to be enjoyed.

FRUIT AND YOGURT SMOOTHIES

Imagine coming home after a long day at school and craving something refreshing and nutritious. That's where fruit and yogurt smoothies come in. They're a perfect snack because they're easy to make, packed with vitamins and protein, and incredibly satisfying. Smoothies are like a hug in a glass— they're creamy, flavorful, and can be customized to suit your taste. Plus, they're a great way to sneak in some extra fruits and veggies without even realizing it.

To make a basic smoothie, you only need a few ingredients: frozen fruit, yogurt, and milk or juice. Start by grabbing your blender. Add about a cup of frozen fruit. You can use anything you like—strawberries, blueberries, mango, you name it. Next, add half a cup of yogurt. Greek yogurt is a great choice because it's thick and adds a nice tangy flavor. Finally, pour in about half a cup of milk or juice to help everything blend smoothly. Blend all the ingredients until you have a creamy, smooth texture. That's it! You've got yourself a delicious, healthy smoothie ready to enjoy.

But why stick with just the basics? Let's explore some creative smoothie combinations that will keep your taste buds excited. For a Berry Blast smoothie, use a mix of strawberries, blueberries, and raspberries. Add vanilla yogurt and a splash of orange juice for a bright, tangy kick. If you're dreaming of a tropical getaway, try the Tropical Paradise smoothie. Combine mango and pineapple with coconut yogurt and coconut water. Each sip will make you feel like you're lounging on a beach. For something a bit more nutritious, the Green Machine smoothie is a fantastic choice. Blend spinach, banana, Greek yogurt, and almond milk. Don't worry, the banana and yogurt mask the spinach taste, giving you a delicious yet healthy snack.

To ensure your smoothies turn out thick and delicious every time, here are some helpful tips. First, always use frozen fruit. It not only keeps your smoothie cold but also gives it a thicker texture without needing ice, which can water it down. If you find your smoothie needs a bit more sweetness, add a touch of honey or agave. They're natural sweeteners that blend well and enhance the flavors. Adjusting the liquid is also key. If your smoothie is too thick, add a bit more milk or juice. If it's too runny, add more frozen fruit or a handful of ice. This way, you can get the consistency just right.

Here's a fun idea: set up a smoothie bar. Lay out different fruits, yogurts, and liquids, and let everyone create their own smoothie masterpiece. It's a great way to get creative and try new combinations. Plus, it's a fun activity to do with friends or family. You can even have themed smoothie days, like tropical or green smoothie day, where you experiment with flavors and see who comes up with the best mix.

Fruit and yogurt smoothies are more than just a snack; they're a refreshing treat that's good for you. They're quick to make, easy to customize, and always delicious. So, grab your blender, pick your favorite ingredients, and blend up a smoothie that's perfect for any time of day. Each sip is a delightful mix of creamy, fruity goodness that will keep you refreshed and energized.

With these tasty and creative after-school munchies, you'll never have to settle for boring snacks again. From mini pizzas to loaded nachos, quick quesadillas to sweet and savory popcorn, and refreshing smoothies, there's something for every craving. These recipes are all about making snack time fun, easy, and delicious. Now, get ready to explore even more delicious and easy-to-make meals in the next chapter.

CHAPTER 6

Dinner Delights

Imagine it's a weeknight, and you've had a long, busy day at school. You're tired, hungry, and the last thing you want to do is spend hours in the kitchen. That's where our dinner delights come in. These recipes are designed to be quick, simple, and incredibly tasty, making dinner time something to look forward to rather than a chore. Whether you're cooking for yourself, your family, or some friends, these meals will make you feel like a culinary rock star.

ONE-POT MAC AND CHEESE

Let's talk about one-pot meals. They're a lifesaver, especially on those nights when you want something delicious without the hassle of a ton of dirty dishes. One-pot mac and cheese is a perfect example. All the ingredients cook together in one pot, making cleanup a breeze. Plus, cooking everything together means the flavors meld in a way that's just irresistible.

You get that creamy, cheesy goodness in every bite, with minimal effort.

One-pot mac and cheese is not just convenient; it's also incredibly delicious. Here's a straightforward recipe to get you started. You'll need some basic ingredients: pasta, milk, cheese, and butter. First, grab a large pot and pour in 4 cups of milk. Bring the milk to a gentle simmer over medium heat, then add 2 cups of uncooked pasta. Stir occasionally to prevent the pasta from sticking to the bottom. Cook until the pasta is tender, which usually takes about 10-12 minutes. Once the pasta is cooked, reduce the heat to low and stir in 2 cups of shredded cheese and 2 tablespoons of butter. Mix until the cheese is fully melted and the sauce is creamy. And there you have it, a delicious pot of mac and cheese, ready to be devoured.

But why stop at just the basics? Let's explore some flavorful variations to make your mac and cheese even more exciting. How about adding some cooked bacon bits? The salty, smoky flavor of bacon complements the creamy cheese beautifully. Or, for a healthier twist, mix in some steamed broccoli or peas. These veggies add a pop of color and a nice crunch, making your meal not only tastier but also more nutritious. You can also experiment with different kinds of cheese. Try a mix of cheddar, mozzarella, and parmesan for a rich, complex flavor. Each type of cheese melts differently, giving your mac and cheese a unique texture and taste.

To ensure your one-pot mac and cheese turns out perfectly creamy and delicious, here are a few tips. First, use high-quality cheese. The better the cheese, the better the flavor and texture of your dish. Avoid pre-shredded cheese if possible, as it often contains anti-caking agents that can affect how the cheese melts. Stir constantly while cooking to prevent the pasta from sticking and to ensure the cheese melts evenly. If your mac and cheese seems too thick, you can add a little more milk to reach your desired creaminess. On the other hand, if it's too runny, simply let it cook a bit longer, stirring frequently, until it thickens up.

One-pot mac and cheese is a fantastic dinner option because it's simple, quick, and incredibly satisfying. The minimal cleanup required means you can spend more time enjoying your meal and less time scrubbing pots and pans. Plus, with so many ways to customize it, you can make it your own every time you cook. So, grab your ingredients, get your pot ready, and let's make some delicious mac and cheese tonight!

INTERACTIVE ACTIVITY: MAC AND CHEESE MASTERPIECE

Create your own mac and cheese masterpiece! Use the base recipe and add your favorite ingredients. Try different cheese combinations, mix in your favorite veggies, or add a protein like chicken or bacon. Write down your favorite combinations and give them fun names. Share your creations with family and friends, and see who can come up with the most delicious and creative mac and cheese dish.

TACO NIGHT: BUILD YOUR OWN TACOS

Imagine it's Friday night, and everyone in the family is ready for some fun. Taco night is the perfect way to bring everyone together for a meal that's both delicious and interactive. The great thing about build-your-own tacos is that they encourage family participation. Everyone gets to be part of the cooking process, from setting up the toppings to assembling their own tacos. This not only makes dinner more enjoyable but also allows everyone to create personalized and creative tacos that suit their tastes. Plus, it's a fantastic way to try new flavors and combinations.

To get started, you'll need some basic taco components. First, choose your protein. Ground beef is a classic choice, but you can also use chicken or beans for a vegetarian option. Cook your protein with taco seasoning for that authentic flavor. Next up are the toppings, and this is where you can really get creative. Shredded lettuce, diced tomatoes, cheese, salsa, and sour cream are must-haves. These toppings add freshness, creaminess, and a bit of tang to your tacos. Finally, you need the shells. Soft tortillas and hard taco shells both work great, so you can offer a variety to suit everyone's preference.

Now let's talk about some unique taco combinations that can make your taco night even more exciting. Fish tacos are a fantastic option. Grill some fish fillets and pair them with a crunchy cabbage slaw and a drizzle of lime crema. The fish adds a light, fresh flavor, while the slaw provides a satisfying crunch. For a vegetarian twist, try veggie tacos. Sauté some bell peppers and onions with black beans. The peppers add sweetness, and the black beans give a hearty texture. If you're in the mood for something different, breakfast tacos are a fun option. Scramble some eggs and add crispy bacon and avocado slices. The creamy avocado pairs beautifully with the salty bacon and fluffy eggs, making for a delightful combination.

To ensure your taco night goes off without a hitch, here are some tips for making it fun and smooth. Start by setting up a taco bar with all the toppings in separate bowls. This makes it easy for everyone to see and choose what they want. Prepping the ingredients in advance can save a lot of time and stress. Chop the veggies, cook the protein, and have everything ready to go before you start assembling. Encourage everyone to try different combinations. Mixing and matching toppings can lead to some surprisingly delicious results. Plus, it's a great way to discover new favorite flavors.

One fun idea to make taco night even more interactive is to have a taco competition. Everyone can create their own unique taco combination, and then you can have a taste test to see whose taco is the best. This adds an element of friendly competition and makes the meal even more enjoyable. You can even come up with fun names for your creations, like "Spicy Fiesta" or "Veggie Delight."

Taco night is not just about the food; it's about the experience. It's a chance to gather around the table, share stories, and enjoy a meal that's both tasty and customizable. With a variety of proteins, toppings, and shells, everyone can create their perfect taco. Whether you stick to classic combinations or venture into new territory with unique flavors, taco night is sure to be a hit. So, gather your ingredients, set up your taco bar, and get ready for a night of delicious, interactive fun.

EASY STIR-FRY WITH VEGGIES AND RICE

Imagine coming home after a long day and needing something quick, nutritious, and delicious. That's where stir-fry comes in. This meal cooks up fast with high heat, locking in all the vibrant flavors and colors of the ingredients. Stir-fry is a fantastic way to pack your dinner full of vegetables while keeping things tasty and fun. Plus, it's super versatile. You can mix and match different veggies, proteins, and sauces to keep things interesting.

To make a basic veggie stir-fry, you'll need some mixed veggies like bell peppers, broccoli, and carrots, along with cooked rice, soy sauce, garlic, and ginger. Start by heating a tablespoon of oil in a large pan or wok over medium-high heat. Once the oil is hot, add minced garlic and grated ginger, letting them sizzle for a few seconds to release their flavors. Next, toss in your veggies. Stir them constantly to ensure even cooking and to prevent them from sticking to the pan. After the veggies are tender-crisp, which should take about 5-7 minutes, add in the cooked rice. Pour soy sauce over the mixture and stir everything together until it's well combined and heated through. And just like that, you've got a delicious stir-fry ready to serve.

But why stop there? Stir-fry is incredibly customizable. For a protein boost, you can add chicken, tofu, or shrimp. These options not only make the dish heartier but also add more flavors and textures. If you're in the mood for a different taste, try using teriyaki, hoisin, or sweet chili sauce instead of soy sauce. Each sauce brings its own unique flavor profile, allowing you to experiment and find your favorite combination. For an extra crunch, toss in some cashews or sesame seeds. These nuts and seeds not only enhance the texture but also add a delightful nutty flavor that complements the veggies and sauce.

To make sure your stir-fry turns out perfect every time, here are a few tips. First, cut your veggies into uniform pieces. This ensures they cook evenly and prevents some pieces from being overcooked while others are still raw. Using high heat is crucial. It allows the veggies to cook quickly, preserving their vibrant colors and crisp textures. Stir constantly to keep everything moving and to prevent burning. Finally, add the sauce towards the end of cooking. This way, it coats all the ingredients without making the dish too soggy.

One of the best things about stir-fry is that it's a great way to use up leftover veggies. Got some bell peppers and snap peas from last night's dinner? Throw them into your stir-fry. The flexibility of this dish makes it not only practical but also economical. You're less likely to waste food, and you get to enjoy a variety of flavors in one meal.

Stir-fry is a quick and nutritious dinner option that's perfect for busy nights. It's packed with vegetables and flavors, making it a satisfying meal that's also good for you. Whether you stick to a basic recipe or get creative with different proteins, sauces, and add-ins, you'll find that stir-fry is a versatile and delicious choice for dinner. So, grab your wok, gather your ingredients, and get ready to stir things up in the kitchen.

SHEET PAN CHICKEN AND VEGGIES

Imagine coming home from school, and you're craving a meal that's both delicious and easy to prepare. Sheet pan chicken and veggies are the answer to your dinnertime woes. This meal is incredibly convenient because it requires minimal dishes to wash. Everything cooks together on one sheet pan, making cleanup a breeze. Plus, cooking everything together allows the flavors to meld, creating a meal that's as tasty as it is simple to make.

To get started with sheet pan chicken and veggies, you'll need some basic ingredients: chicken thighs or breasts, mixed veggies like potatoes, carrots, and broccoli, olive oil, and your favorite seasonings. Begin by preheating your oven to 400°F (200°C). While the oven heats up, arrange the chicken and veggies on a large sheet pan. Drizzle everything with olive oil, then sprinkle with salt, pepper, and any other seasonings you like. Toss the veggies to ensure they're evenly coated. Place the sheet pan in the oven and bake for about 30-40 minutes, or until the chicken is cooked through and the veggies are tender. The result is a hearty, balanced dinner that's ready in no time.

Now, let's talk about some ways to keep your sheet pan meals interesting with different seasoning and veggie combinations. For a fresh and zesty twist, try a Lemon Garlic variation. Arrange lemon slices, minced garlic, and sprigs of rosemary around the chicken and veggies before baking. The lemon and garlic infuse the dish with a bright, aromatic flavor. If you're in the mood for something smoky and sweet, a BBQ version is perfect. Use BBQ sauce to marinate the chicken, and add sweet potatoes and corn to the veggie mix. The BBQ sauce caramelizes as it bakes, creating a delicious glaze. For a taste of Italy, go with an Italian seasoning blend. Toss the chicken and veggies with Italian seasoning, cherry tomatoes, and zucchini. The herbs and tomatoes create a rich, savory flavor that's hard to resist.

To ensure your sheet pan chicken and veggies turn out perfectly every time, here are some helpful tips. Start by cutting the veggies into similar-sized pieces. This ensures they cook evenly, so you don't end up with some undercooked and others overdone. Marinating the chicken beforehand can add extra flavor and tenderness. Simply coat the chicken in your chosen marinade and let it sit in the fridge for at least 30 minutes before cooking. Finally, rotate the pan halfway through cooking. This helps everything cook evenly and prevents any hotspots in the oven from overcooking one side of the dish.

One of the great things about sheet pan meals is their flexibility. You can easily swap out veggies based on what you have on hand or what's in season. Bell peppers, Brussels sprouts, and butternut squash are all excellent additions. You can also experiment with different proteins. Try using boneless pork chops or even firm tofu for a vegetarian option. The possibilities are endless, and each variation brings a new flavor profile to your dinner table.

Sheet pan chicken and veggies are not just convenient; they're also a fantastic way to enjoy a balanced, nutritious meal. The combination of protein, vegetables, and healthy fats from the olive oil makes this dish both satisfying and good for you. Plus, with the variety of seasoning options, you can keep your dinners exciting and full of flavor. So, grab your sheet pan, pick your favorite veggies and seasonings, and get ready to enjoy a delicious, hassle-free dinner tonight.

SPAGHETTI AND MEATBALLS MADE SIMPLE

Imagine coming home to the comforting aroma of spaghetti and meatballs simmering on the stove. This classic dish is not only delicious but also a fantastic way for kids and teens to learn some basic cooking skills. It combines simple ingredients to create a hearty meal that everyone loves. Plus, making spaghetti and meatballs from scratch is a great way to practice boiling and sautéing, two essential techniques in the kitchen.

To get started, you'll need some ground beef or turkey, breadcrumbs, an egg, spaghetti, and marinara sauce. First, let's make the meatballs. In a large bowl, combine one pound of ground meat with half a cup of breadcrumbs, one beaten egg, and a pinch of salt and pepper. Mix everything together until well combined. Then, form the mixture into small balls, about the size of a ping pong ball. Heat a tablespoon of oil in a large skillet over medium heat. Add the meatballs and cook them until they're browned on all sides and cooked through, which should take about 10 minutes. While the meatballs are cooking, bring a large pot of salted water to a boil and cook the spaghetti according to the package instructions. Once the pasta is done, drain it and set it aside.

After the meatballs are cooked, remove them from the skillet and set them aside. In the same skillet, pour in a jar of marinara sauce. Add the meatballs back to the skillet and let them simmer in the sauce for about 10 minutes. This allows the flavors to meld together, making the meatballs even more delicious. Finally, toss the cooked spaghetti with the sauce and meatballs, and serve hot. This simple recipe results in a comforting, satisfying meal that's perfect for any night of the week.

But why stick to just one version of spaghetti and meatballs? There are plenty of ways to customize this dish to suit your tastes. For a burst of flavor, try adding some herbs and spices to the meatball mixture. A teaspoon of dried basil, oregano, or garlic powder can make a big difference. You can also experiment with different types of meat. Ground pork or chicken are great alternatives to beef, and for a vegetarian option, you can use plant-based meat substitutes or even lentils. If you're feeling adventurous, you can make your own marinara sauce using fresh tomatoes, garlic, onions, and herbs. Simply sauté the garlic and onions, add chopped tomatoes, and let it simmer until it thickens. Stir in some fresh basil for a delicious, homemade touch.

To ensure your spaghetti and meatballs turn out perfect every time, here are some helpful tips. First, make sure the meatballs are cooked until they're nicely browned on the outside and fully cooked on the inside. This not only ensures they're safe to eat but also gives them a delicious, caramelized flavor. When cooking the pasta, use plenty of salted water. The salt enhances the flavor of the pasta, making the whole dish more delicious. Finally, let the meatballs simmer in the sauce for a while. This infuses the sauce with the rich flavors of the meatballs and makes the dish even more flavorful.

Spaghetti and meatballs are a classic for a reason. They're delicious, comforting, and a great way to learn some basic cooking skills. With simple ingredients and straightforward instructions, you can create a meal that's both satisfying and impressive. So, grab your ingredients, roll up your sleeves, and get ready to make some delicious spaghetti and meatballs tonight.

Dinner time doesn't have to be complicated or stressful. With these easy and tasty recipes, you can enjoy a variety of delicious meals without spending hours in the kitchen. From one-pot mac and cheese to build-your-own tacos, quick stir-fries, and sheet pan dinners, there's something for everyone. Each dish is designed to be simple, flavorful, and fun to make. So, whether you're cooking for yourself, your family, or your friends, you're sure to impress with these dinner delights. Ready to discover more tasty recipes? Let's move on to the next chapter and explore some sweet treats and desserts that will satisfy your sweet tooth.

CHAPTER 7

Sweet Treats

Imagine this: It's the weekend, and you've got friends coming over for a sleepover. You all want to do something fun and delicious, so you decide to set up an ice cream sundae bar. The excitement is palpable as you gather around, ready to create your own ice cream masterpieces. Setting up a sundae bar is not just about the ice cream; it's about the sheer joy of picking and choosing your favorite toppings, mixing and matching flavors, and creating something unique and delicious. It's the perfect way to end a meal, celebrate a birthday, or simply have a fun and interactive dessert experience with friends and family.

DIY ICE CREAM SUNDAE BAR

Setting up an ice cream sundae bar is a fantastic way to encourage creativity and personalization. Everyone gets to be their own chef, choosing from a variety of ice cream flavors, toppings, and sauces to create a dessert that's uniquely theirs. It's a great activity for parties or family gatherings because it gets everyone involved and excited. Plus, there's something magical about seeing a table filled with colorful toppings and delicious ice cream, just waiting to be transformed into a sundae masterpiece.

Let's start with the basics of setting up your sundae bar. You'll need a few essential components to get started. First, choose your ice cream flavors. Classic options like vanilla, chocolate, and strawberry are always a hit, but feel free to get creative with flavors like mint chocolate chip, cookies and cream, or even a fun seasonal flavor like pumpkin spice. Next, you'll need a variety of toppings. Think sprinkles, chocolate chips, and fresh fruit like banana slices, berries, and mango chunks. Don't forget the sauces! Chocolate syrup, caramel, and strawberry sauce are must-haves for any sundae bar.

Once you have your essentials, it's time to get creative with some unique topping ideas. Crushed cookies like Oreos or chocolate chip cookies add a delightful crunch. Gummy bears and mini marshmallows bring a fun, playful element to your sundaes. Nuts like almonds, peanuts, and walnuts add a nice contrast to the sweetness of the ice cream. The possibilities are endless, and the best part is that you can mix and match to your heart's content.

Presentation is key when it comes to making your sundaes visually appealing. Start by layering your toppings for a colorful effect. For example, place a scoop of vanilla ice cream in a clear bowl or glass, add a layer of fresh strawberries, then a drizzle of chocolate syrup, followed by a sprinkle of rainbow sprinkles. Keep layering until your bowl is full, and don't forget to add a cherry on top for that classic sundae look.

Using clear bowls or glasses is a great way to showcase the beautiful layers and colors of your sundae, making it look as good as it tastes.

Here's a quick checklist to help you set up your sundae bar:

SUNDAE BAR CHECKLIST

- **Ice Cream Flavors:** Vanilla, chocolate, strawberry, mint chocolate chip, cookies and cream
- **Toppings:** Sprinkles, chocolate chips, crushed cookies, gummy bears, mini marshmallows, nuts (almonds, peanuts, walnuts), fresh fruit (banana slices, berries, mango chunks)
- **Sauces:** Chocolate syrup, caramel, strawberry sauce
- **Extras:** Whipped cream, maraschino cherries
- **Tools:** Bowls, spoons, ice cream scoops, napkins

Having a sundae bar is all about making dessert time fun and interactive. It allows everyone to get involved and create something they'll love. So, gather your friends, set up your sundae bar, and get ready to enjoy some delicious, personalized ice cream sundaes. It's the perfect way to bring a little extra joy to any gathering.

CHOCOLATE-DIPPED FRUITS

Imagine a treat that combines the natural sweetness of fruit with the rich, indulgent taste of chocolate. Chocolate-dipped fruits are exactly that—a delicious and healthy dessert option that's incredibly easy to make. Imagine biting into a juicy strawberry coated in smooth, velvety chocolate. The contrast between the fresh fruit and the rich chocolate makes each bite a delightful experience. Plus, they're visually appealing, making them perfect for special occasions or just as a fun snack. Whether you're enjoying them at a party or making them for a family dessert, chocolate-dipped fruits are always a hit.

To get started, you'll need some basic ingredients: assorted fruits like strawberries, bananas, and apple slices, and chocolate chips. You can choose dark chocolate, milk chocolate, or white chocolate, depending on your preference. Optional toppings like chopped nuts or coconut flakes can add extra flavor and texture. Begin by washing and thoroughly drying your fruits. It's important to dry them well because water can prevent the chocolate from sticking properly. Next, melt your chocolate. You can do this using a double boiler or simply by microwaving the chocolate chips in short bursts, stirring in between to ensure it melts evenly.

Once your chocolate is melted and smooth, it's time to dip the fruits. Hold each piece of fruit by the stem or use a fork or skewer to dip it into the chocolate, making sure it's evenly coated. Let any excess chocolate drip off, then place the dipped fruit on a piece of parchment paper to set. If you're using toppings, sprinkle them on while the chocolate is still wet so they stick. Repeat this process until all your fruits are dipped and decorated. Let the chocolate set at room temperature or speed up the process by placing the fruits in the refrigerator.

For a twist on the classic, try some creative flavor combinations. Dark chocolate pairs beautifully with strawberries, offering a rich and slightly bitter contrast to the sweet fruit. White chocolate with pineapple is another fantastic combination, as the creamy sweetness of the white chocolate complements the tartness of the pineapple. If you're a fan of milk chocolate, try dipping apple slices for a treat that's reminiscent of caramel apples but with a chocolatey twist. These combinations not only taste amazing but also look stunning, making them perfect for impressing your friends and family.

Decorating your chocolate-dipped fruits can be just as fun as making them. For an elegant touch, try drizzling a contrasting chocolate over the dipped fruits. For example, you can use a spoon to drizzle white chocolate over dark chocolate-dipped strawberries, creating a beautiful pattern. If you're in the mood for something a bit more festive, sprinkle your fruits with colorful sprinkles or edible glitter. Chopped nuts like almonds, peanuts, or walnuts add a nice crunch and extra flavor. Coconut flakes are another great option, adding a tropical twist to your treats. The key is to have fun and get creative with your decorations.

Here's a quick tip: if you're making chocolate-dipped fruits for a party or special occasion, set up a dipping station where everyone can dip and decorate their own fruits. Lay out bowls of melted chocolate, assorted fruits, and a variety of toppings. This not only makes the process interactive and fun but also allows everyone to create their perfect chocolate-dipped treat. It's a great way to get everyone involved and make the experience even more enjoyable.

Chocolate-dipped fruits are a fantastic way to enjoy a healthy, delicious dessert that's both easy to make and fun to eat. The combination of fresh fruit and rich chocolate is a classic that never gets old. So, gather your ingredients, melt some chocolate, and get ready to dip and decorate to your heart's content. Each bite will be a delightful explosion of flavors, making these treats a favorite for any occasion.

NO-BAKE COOKIES

Imagine coming home from school and craving something sweet, but you don't want to wait for the oven to preheat or spend ages measuring and mixing. That's where no-bake cookies come in. These delightful treats are quick and easy to make, requiring no oven and minimal preparation. They're perfect for those moments when you need a delicious dessert in a hurry. With just a few simple ingredients, you can whip up a batch of cookies that are ready to eat in no time. No-bake cookies are the ultimate solution for satisfying your sweet tooth without the hassle of baking.

To get started with a basic no-bake cookie recipe, you'll need some oats, peanut butter, honey, and cocoa powder. These ingredients are likely already in your pantry, making this recipe even more convenient. Begin by grabbing a mixing bowl and adding one cup of oats. Next, add half a cup of peanut butter. If your peanut butter is a bit thick, you can microwave it for a few seconds to make it easier to mix. Now, pour in a third of a cup of honey. This acts as a natural sweetener and helps bind the ingredients together. Finally, add two tablespoons of cocoa powder for that rich, chocolatey flavor. Mix everything until well combined. Once your mixture is ready, scoop out small portions and shape them into cookies. Place the cookies on a piece of parchment paper and refrigerate them for about an hour to set. There you have it—delicious no-bake cookies ready to enjoy.

But why stop at the basics? There are so many ways to customize no-bake cookies to suit your taste. For a tropical twist, try adding shredded coconut and chocolate chips to the mixture. The coconut adds a chewy texture and pairs perfectly with the chocolate. If you're a fan of fruity flavors, mix in some dried cranberries and almond butter instead of peanut butter. The cranberries add a burst of tartness, while the almond butter provides a rich, nutty flavor. For those who love a bit of indulgence, try adding Nutella and chopped hazelnuts. The Nutella gives the cookies a creamy, chocolatey taste, while the hazelnuts add a satisfying crunch. Each variation brings a unique flavor and texture, making your no-bake cookies even more enjoyable.

To ensure your no-bake cookies turn out perfectly every time, here are a few tips. First, use quick oats instead of old-fashioned oats. Quick oats are smaller and softer, giving your cookies a better texture. Second, make sure to allow adequate time for the cookies to set in the refrigerator. This helps them firm up and hold their shape. If you're in a hurry, you can speed up the process by placing them in the freezer for about 30 minutes. Lastly, don't forget to add a pinch of salt to the mixture. Salt enhances the flavors and balances the sweetness of the cookies, making them taste even better.

No-bake cookies are not just about convenience; they're also about creativity and fun. You can experiment with different ingredients and flavors to create your perfect cookie. The possibilities are endless, and part of the fun is discovering new combinations that you love. Plus, they're a great way to get kids involved in the kitchen. Since there's no need for an oven, it's a safe and easy recipe for young chefs to make on their own or with a little help from an adult.

So, gather your ingredients, mix up a batch, and enjoy the delicious, no-fuss goodness of no-bake cookies. Each bite will be a delightful reminder that sometimes the simplest recipes are the most satisfying. Whether you stick to the classic recipe or venture into new flavor combinations, you'll find that no-bake cookies are a quick and easy dessert option that everyone will love.

FUNFETTI CUPCAKES

Imagine walking into a room filled with the aroma of freshly baked cupcakes, each one topped with a swirl of colorful frosting and a sprinkle of edible confetti. That's the magic of funfetti cupcakes! These delightful treats are not just delicious; they're a visual feast that screams celebration. Bright colors make them incredibly appealing, and they're perfect for birthdays, parties, or any occasion that calls for a bit of festivity. Every bite is a burst of joy, thanks to the vibrant sprinkles mixed into the batter. They're like little edible fireworks that make every moment special.

Making funfetti cupcakes from scratch is easier than you might think. You'll need some basic ingredients: flour, sugar, eggs, butter, and, of course, sprinkles. Start by preheating your oven to 350°F (175°C) and lining a cupcake tin with paper liners. In a mixing bowl, cream together one cup of softened butter and one and a half cups of sugar until light and fluffy. Add in three large eggs, one at a time, beating well after each addition. Next, mix in two teaspoons of vanilla extract. In another bowl, whisk together two and a half cups of flour, two and a half teaspoons of baking powder, and half a teaspoon of salt. Gradually add the dry ingredients to the wet ingredients, alternating with one cup of milk, beginning and ending with the flour mixture. Finally, fold in half a cup of colorful sprinkles. Be gentle to avoid overmixing, as this can cause the sprinkles to bleed. Fill each cupcake liner about two-thirds full with batter and bake for 18-20 minutes, or until a toothpick inserted into the center comes out clean. Let the cupcakes cool in the pan for a few minutes before transferring them to a wire rack to cool completely.

Now comes the fun part—decorating your cupcakes! There are countless ways to make your funfetti cupcakes look as amazing as they taste. Start with different colored frosting to match the theme of your celebration. You can use a piping bag to create beautiful swirls or simply spread the frosting with a spatula for a rustic look. Add more sprinkles on top for an extra pop of color. Edible glitter can make your cupcakes sparkle, adding a touch of magic to each bite. Decorative candies, like mini marshmallows or candy pearls, can also add a whimsical touch. The key is to have fun and let your creativity shine.

To ensure your cupcakes turn out light and fluffy, here are a few tips. First, avoid overmixing the batter. Once the flour is added, mix just until combined to keep the texture tender. Overmixing can lead to dense, tough cupcakes. Second, fill your cupcake liners evenly. Using an ice cream scoop can help you measure the batter consistently, ensuring that each cupcake bakes evenly. Finally, check for doneness with a toothpick. Insert it into the center of a cupcake; if it comes out clean or with a few crumbs, they're ready. If there's still wet batter, give them a couple more minutes in the oven.

You can get creative with the flavors too. Try adding a hint of almond extract for a nutty twist or a touch of lemon zest for a refreshing citrus flavor. The possibilities are endless, and experimenting with different ingredients can make baking even more enjoyable. Funfetti cupcakes are not just a treat; they're an experience that brings joy and excitement to any celebration. So, gather your ingredients, preheat your oven, and get ready to bake a batch of cupcakes that are as delightful to look at as they are to eat. Each bite will be a celebration of flavors and colors, making these cupcakes a favorite for any occasion.

DIY S'MORES INDOORS

Imagine this: It's a rainy evening, and you're craving something sweet and comforting. You don't need a campfire to enjoy the classic treat of s'mores. Making s'mores indoors is a fun and effortless dessert activity that you can do right in your kitchen. All you need are a few common kitchen appliances, like an oven or a microwave, to recreate that gooey, chocolatey goodness. It's a fantastic way to bring the joy of camping indoors, perfect for a cozy night with family or friends.

To make s'mores indoors, you'll need three basic ingredients: graham crackers, marshmallows, and chocolate bars. Start by breaking your graham crackers in half to create two squares. Place one square on a baking sheet and top it with a piece of chocolate. Next, add a marshmallow on top of the chocolate. If you're using an oven, preheat it to 350°F (175°C). Once it's ready, pop the baking sheet in and let the marshmallows heat until they're melted and gooey, which should take about 5 minutes. If you're using a microwave, assemble the s'mores on a microwave-safe plate and heat them on high for about 15-20 seconds. Once the marshmallows are perfectly gooey, top them with the other graham cracker square and press down gently to create your s'more. Congratulations, you've just made a delicious indoor s'more!

But why stick to the basics when you can get creative with your s'mores? Try using flavored marshmallows like strawberry or caramel for a unique twist. Adding a layer of peanut butter or Nutella between the chocolate and marshmallow can elevate your s'mores to a whole new level of deliciousness. And don't be afraid to experiment with different types of chocolate. White chocolate can add a creamy sweetness, while dark chocolate offers a rich, slightly bitter contrast to the sweet marshmallow. These variations not only taste amazing but also add a fun element of surprise to your s'mores-making experience.

Here are some tips to ensure your s'mores turn out delicious and gooey every time. First, make sure to heat the marshmallows evenly. If you're using an oven, place the baking sheet on the middle rack to ensure even heating. If you're using a microwave, keep an eye on the marshmallows as they can puff up quickly. Once they're melted and gooey, it's crucial to assemble your s'mores quickly to keep the chocolate melted and the marshmallow soft. For an extra touch of authenticity, use a broiler to toast the marshmallows. Simply place the assembled s'mores under the broiler for a few seconds until the marshmallows are golden brown and slightly crispy on the outside. Just be careful not to let them burn!

Making s'mores indoors is all about bringing that campfire magic into your home. It's a simple, fun, and delicious way to enjoy a classic treat without needing to venture outdoors. So, gather your ingredients, preheat your oven or microwave, and get ready to make some gooey, chocolatey s'mores. Each bite will transport you to a cozy campfire, even if you're just sitting in your kitchen. The possibilities are endless, and the fun is guaranteed.

CHAPTER 8

Party Time!

Imagine this: You're planning a party, and you want the food to be as fun and exciting as the event itself. You need something that's easy to eat, customizable, and guaranteed to be a hit with everyone. Enter mini sliders! These bite-sized burgers are perfect for any party. They're easy to handle, pack a punch of flavor, and can be customized to suit any taste. Whether you're hosting a birthday bash, a sleepover, or just a fun get-together, mini sliders are the ultimate crowd-pleaser.

MINI SLIDERS FOR THE CROWD

Mini sliders are the perfect party food for several reasons. First, they're easy to eat and handle. Unlike big burgers that can be messy, sliders are small enough to fit comfortably in your hand. This makes them ideal for parties where guests might be mingling or playing games. Plus, they're super fun to customize. You can create a variety of sliders with different fillings, ensuring there's something for everyone. From classic beef sliders to creative veggie and breakfast options, the possibilities are endless.

Let's start with a basic mini slider recipe that's both simple and delicious. You'll need mini burger buns, ground beef or turkey, cheese, lettuce, and tomato. First, form small patties from the ground beef or turkey. Season them with a bit of salt and pepper. Heat a skillet or grill over medium heat and cook the patties until they're browned on the outside and cooked through on the inside. This should take about 3-4 minutes per side. While the patties are cooking, prepare your buns and toppings. Slice the mini buns in half and get the cheese, lettuce, and tomato ready. Once the patties are done, assemble the sliders by placing a patty on the bottom half of the bun, adding a slice of cheese, a piece of lettuce, and a tomato slice. Top it off with the other half of the bun, and you're ready to serve!

Now that you have the basics down, let's get creative with some variations. How about BBQ chicken sliders? These are made with shredded chicken mixed with BBQ sauce and topped with coleslaw. The combination of tangy BBQ sauce and crunchy coleslaw is irresistible. To make these, simply cook and shred some chicken, mix it with your favorite BBQ sauce, and assemble the sliders with the chicken and coleslaw. Another great option is veggie sliders. These can be made with black bean patties, avocado, and salsa. They're not only delicious but also a great option for vegetarians. To make the black bean patties, mash some black beans with breadcrumbs, an egg, and your favorite spices. Form small patties and cook them in a skillet until crispy on the outside.

Assemble the sliders with the black bean patties, avocado slices, and a spoonful of salsa.

For a fun twist, try making breakfast sliders. These are perfect for brunch parties or sleepovers. Imagine a slider with scrambled eggs, crispy bacon, and melted cheddar cheese. To make these, cook some scrambled eggs and bacon. Assemble the sliders with the scrambled eggs, a slice of bacon, and a piece of cheddar cheese. The combination of savory bacon, creamy eggs, and sharp cheddar is sure to be a hit.

When serving sliders at a party, it's important to keep them warm and fresh. One great tip is to use a slow cooker. After assembling the sliders, place them in a slow cooker set to the "warm" setting. This keeps them at the perfect temperature without drying them out. Another tip is to assemble the sliders just before serving. This ensures that the buns stay soft and the ingredients are fresh. For added fun, use decorative toothpicks to hold the sliders together. Not only do they make the sliders easier to handle, but they also add a festive touch to your party spread.

Mini sliders are a fantastic addition to any party. They're easy to make, fun to customize, and a guaranteed crowd-pleaser. So, gather your ingredients, fire up the grill, and get ready to serve up some delicious mini sliders that your guests will love.

RAINBOW VEGGIE PLATTER

Imagine walking into a party and seeing a vibrant, colorful display of fresh vegetables arranged in a beautiful pattern. That's the magic of a rainbow veggie platter. Not only is it visually stunning, but it's also a healthy and delicious option that encourages everyone to eat their veggies. A rainbow veggie platter is perfect for parties because it's easy to prepare, serve, and enjoy. Plus, it adds a burst of color to any table, making it instantly more inviting.

Creating a rainbow veggie platter is all about variety and presentation. Start by gathering an assortment of colorful vegetables. Think bright bell peppers in red, yellow, and orange; crisp carrots sliced into sticks; juicy cherry tomatoes; and cool cucumber slices. Wash all the vegetables thoroughly and cut them into bite-sized pieces. The key is to have a mix of textures and colors that not only look good together but also taste great. Once you've prepped your veggies, it's time to arrange them on a large, flat platter or tray.

To make your platter truly stand out, arrange the vegetables in a rainbow pattern. Start with red bell peppers, followed by orange carrots, yellow bell peppers, green cucumber slices, and ending with purple cauliflower or radishes. This creates a visually appealing gradient that's sure to catch everyone's eye. Grouping the vegetables by color not only looks fantastic but also makes it easy for guests to pick their favorites. You can even add some mini heirloom tomatoes or broccolini for extra flair. The result is a platter that's as beautiful as it is healthy.

No veggie platter is complete without delicious dips to accompany it. Classic ranch dip is always a hit. You can make a healthier version by using Greek yogurt instead of sour cream. Simply mix Greek yogurt with a bit of dill, garlic powder, and a pinch of salt. Another great option is hummus. Made from chickpeas, tahini, lemon juice, and garlic, it's creamy and flavorful. For a bit of a twist, try guacamole. Mashing ripe avocados with lime juice and cilantro creates a smooth, rich dip that pairs perfectly with the crunchy veggies.

Presentation is everything when it comes to a rainbow veggie platter. Use a large, flat platter or tray to give yourself plenty of space to arrange the vegetables. Start by placing small bowls of your dips in the center of the platter. This not only makes it easy for guests to access the dips but also serves as the focal point of the arrangement. Then, work your way outwards, placing the vegetables in groups based on their color. This creates a stunning visual effect and makes the platter look abundant and inviting.

To take your presentation to the next level, add some decorative elements. Edible flowers or fresh herbs like dill or parsley can add a touch of elegance and make your platter look even more appetizing. You can also garnish the dips with a drizzle of olive oil or a sprinkle of paprika for an extra pop of color. These little touches make a big difference and show that you've put thought and effort into your creation.

Creating a rainbow veggie platter is not just about making something that looks good; it's about encouraging healthy eating in a fun and appealing way. By presenting a variety of colorful vegetables and tasty dips, you're making it easy for everyone to enjoy a nutritious snack. It's a great way to add a healthy option to your party spread without sacrificing flavor or fun. So, next time you're planning a party, consider making a rainbow veggie platter. It's sure to be a hit with guests of all ages.

DIY PIZZA PARTY

Imagine inviting your friends over for a party where everyone gets to be a chef, creating their own pizza masterpieces. Setting up a DIY pizza station is not only fun but also interactive, encouraging everyone to get involved and express their creativity. Each guest can customize their pizza with their favorite toppings, making it a unique and personal experience. This hands-on activity turns a simple meal into an exciting event, where everyone can enjoy their personalized creations.

Let's start with a basic pizza dough recipe that's easy to make from scratch. You'll need flour, yeast, warm water, olive oil, and salt. Begin by dissolving one teaspoon of yeast in one and a half cups of warm water. Let it sit for about five minutes until it becomes frothy. In a large mixing bowl, combine three cups of all-purpose flour with a teaspoon of salt. Make a well in the center and pour in the yeast mixture along with two tablespoons of olive oil. Mix everything together until it forms a dough. Turn the dough onto a floured surface and knead it for about ten minutes until it's smooth and elastic. Place the dough in a lightly oiled bowl, cover it with a damp cloth, and let it rise in a warm place for about an hour, or until it doubles in size. Once risen, divide the dough into individual portions, ready for your guests to roll out and top as they wish.

When it comes to toppings, the sky's the limit. Start with a variety of sauces to cater to different tastes. Classic tomato sauce is a must, but you can also offer pesto and Alfredo sauce for those who like something different. Cheese is another essential component, so provide options like mozzarella, cheddar, and feta. For proteins, think beyond just pepperoni. Offer sausage, grilled chicken, and even vegetarian options like tofu. Veggies add color and flavor to pizzas, so include bell peppers, mushrooms, spinach, and olives. Don't forget the extras like pineapple for a sweet touch, fresh basil for a burst of flavor, and red pepper flakes for a bit of heat. By providing a wide range of toppings, you ensure that there's something for everyone, making the pizza-making process even more enjoyable.

Setting up your DIY pizza station involves a bit of organization to keep things running smoothly. Start by prepping and organizing all the toppings in separate bowls. This makes it easy for guests to see all their options and choose their favorites. Provide rolling pins and baking sheets for each guest so they can roll out their dough and assemble their pizzas. A baking station with a preheated oven or a pizza stone is essential for quick and even cooking. If you have a pizza peel, it can make transferring the pizzas to the oven easier. Make sure to preheat the oven to a high temperature, around 450°F (230°C), to get that perfect, crispy crust.

To add a fun twist, you can set up a friendly competition. Have everyone create their pizza and then vote on the most creative, the best-looking, or the most delicious one. This adds an element of excitement and encourages everyone to put a bit more thought into their creations. You can even offer small prizes for the winners, like a special dessert or a fun kitchen gadget. This not only makes the party more engaging but also gives everyone a chance to show off their culinary skills.

A DIY pizza party is a fantastic way to bring people together, allowing everyone to get hands-on and make something delicious. It's an activity that combines creativity, fun, and food, making it perfect for any occasion. So, gather your ingredients, set up your pizza station, and get ready for a pizza-making adventure that your guests will remember and enjoy.

FUN PUNCH AND MOCKTAILS

Imagine walking into a party where the drinks are as exciting as the food. Punch and mocktails are fantastic non-alcoholic drink options that are refreshing and enjoyable for all ages. They can be made in large batches, making them perfect for easy serving at parties. The vibrant colors and delicious flavors make them a hit with everyone. Plus, they offer a chance for you to get creative and have some fun with your drink-making skills.

Let's start with a basic punch recipe that's simple yet delicious. You'll need some fruit juice, soda or sparkling water, and fresh fruit slices. Begin by pouring your favorite fruit juice into a large punch bowl. You can use any juice you like—orange, apple, pineapple, or a mix of several. Next, add an equal amount of soda or sparkling water. This gives the punch a nice fizzy texture. Finally, toss in some fresh fruit slices. Oranges, lemons, and berries work great and add a burst of color and flavor. Add some ice to keep the punch chilled, and give it a good stir. There you have it—a refreshing party punch that's sure to please.

But why stop at just one type of punch when you can offer a variety of mocktails to cater to different tastes? One fun option is a Virgin Mojito. To make this, squeeze the juice of a few limes into a glass, add a handful of fresh mint leaves, and top it off with soda water. Stir gently to mix the flavors, and you've got a zesty, refreshing drink. For something fruity, try a Berry Fizz. Mix some mixed berry juice with lemon-lime soda and add a handful of fresh berries. The combination of sweet berries and fizzy soda is irresistible. If you're in the mood for a tropical vibe, whip up a Tropical Paradise mocktail. Combine pineapple juice, coconut water, and a splash of grenadine. The result is a drink that tastes like a vacation in a glass.

Presentation is key when serving punch and mocktails. Using colorful straws and umbrellas can instantly make your drinks more fun and festive. Think about garnishing each glass with fresh fruit slices or mint sprigs. Not only does this add extra flavor, but it also makes the drinks look more appealing. Serving your punch and mocktails in clear glasses or punch cups is another great idea. This way, the vibrant colors of the drinks are showcased, making them even more inviting. You can even use a large, clear punch bowl with a ladle, so guests can serve themselves and see all the beautiful fruit slices floating in the punch.

Here's a tip to take your punch presentation to the next level: make ice cubes with pieces of fruit inside. Simply place small fruit pieces like berries or citrus slices into ice cube trays, fill with water, and freeze. When you add these fruity ice cubes to your punch, they not only keep the drink cold but also add a fun visual element as they float around. Plus, as the ice melts, it releases the fruit flavors into the punch, making it even more delicious.

Creating punch and mocktails for your party is not just about quenching thirst; it's about adding an extra layer of fun and creativity to your event. Whether you stick to a classic punch or experiment with different mocktail recipes, you'll find that these drinks are a hit with guests of all ages. So, gather your ingredients, set up your drink station, and get ready to serve up some refreshing and delightful beverages that will make your party even more memorable.

CUPCAKE DECORATING EXTRAVAGANZA

Imagine walking into a party where a whole table is dedicated to decorating cupcakes. It's not just a treat for your taste buds but also a canvas for your creativity. Setting up a cupcake decorating station at your party allows your guests to personalize their own cupcakes, making the experience both fun and interactive. It's a fantastic way to encourage artistic expression and let everyone's imagination run wild. Each guest can choose their favorite flavors, frostings, and toppings, creating a unique cupcake that reflects their personality.

To get started, you'll need a simple and foolproof recipe for classic vanilla cupcakes. The ingredients are straightforward: flour, sugar, eggs, butter, and vanilla extract. Begin by preheating your oven to 350°F (175°C) and lining a cupcake tray with paper liners. In a large mixing bowl, cream together one cup of softened butter and two cups of sugar until light and fluffy. Add four eggs, one at a time, beating well after each

addition. Mix in two teaspoons of vanilla extract. In a separate bowl, combine three cups of flour with one tablespoon of baking powder. Gradually add the dry ingredients to the wet mixture, alternating with one cup of milk, starting and ending with the flour mixture. Once everything is well combined, fill the cupcake liners about two-thirds full with the batter. Bake for 18-20 minutes, or until a toothpick inserted into the center comes out clean. Let the cupcakes cool completely before decorating.

Now, let's talk about the fun part—frosting and decorating your cupcakes. Offer a variety of frosting options to cater to different tastes. Classic vanilla buttercream is a favorite for its smooth and creamy texture. For chocolate lovers, a rich chocolate ganache is irresistible. If you're looking for something a bit tangier, cream cheese frosting is a great choice. To make the decorating process even more exciting, provide an array of decorations. Sprinkles in all shapes and colors add a festive touch. Edible glitter can make your cupcakes sparkle, and colored sugars can create beautiful designs. For toppings, consider mini marshmallows, chocolate chips, and fresh fruit slices. Each guest can mix and match these elements to create their perfect cupcake.

Setting up your cupcake decorating station requires a bit of planning to ensure everything runs smoothly. Start by prepping all your decorating supplies before the party begins. Fill piping bags with different frosting flavors and provide a variety of piping tips so guests can experiment with different designs. Lay out all the decorations in small bowls for easy access. It's also a good idea to set up a designated area with plenty of space for guests to decorate their cupcakes comfortably. Cover the table with a disposable tablecloth or parchment paper to make cleanup easier. Provide plenty of napkins and wet wipes to handle any frosting mishaps.

For an added layer of fun, consider incorporating a cupcake decorating contest. Guests can vote on the most creative, the most colorful, or the most appetizing cupcake. Offer small prizes for the winners, such as a special baking tool or a box of gourmet sprinkles. This adds an element of friendly competition and encourages everyone to put a bit more effort into their creations.

A cupcake decorating station is more than just a party activity; it's an opportunity for everyone to showcase their creativity and enjoy a delicious treat. It's perfect for birthdays, sleepovers, or any celebration where you want to add a touch of sweetness and fun. So, gather your ingredients, set up your station, and get ready for a cupcake decorating extravaganza that your guests will love.

With all these amazing ideas, your parties are sure to be a hit. From mini sliders to rainbow veggie platters, DIY pizzas to fun drinks, and now cupcake decorating, you've got everything you need to throw the best party ever. Next up, we'll explore how to turn your cooking skills into a fun challenge, perfect for any gathering. Stay tuned!

CHAPTER 9

Cooking Challenges and Adventures

Imagine this: it's a rainy afternoon, and you're stuck inside with nothing to do. You head to the kitchen, looking for a snack, but then you notice a few random ingredients sitting on the counter. Suddenly, an idea sparks—why not turn this into a cooking challenge? Welcome to the Mystery Ingredient Challenge, a fun and creative way to experiment in the kitchen and put your culinary skills to the test.

MYSTERY INGREDIENT CHALLENGE

The Mystery Ingredient Challenge is all about thinking outside the box and using your imagination. It's a game where you take a few unexpected ingredients and create something delicious. This activity encourages you to be adaptable and solve problems on the fly. You'll learn how to balance flavors, textures, and colors, all while having a blast in the kitchen. It's like being on a cooking show, but in your own home!

Setting up a Mystery Ingredient Challenge is easy and exciting. Start by selecting a few mystery ingredients. These could be anything from apples and cheddar cheese to spinach and strawberries. The key is to choose ingredients that you wouldn't normally think to pair together. You can ask a family member or friend to pick the ingredients for you to make it even more surprising. Once you have your mystery ingredients, set a time limit for creating your dish. It could be 30 minutes or an hour, depending on how complex you want the challenge to be. Use pantry staples like salt, pepper, and olive oil to complement the mystery ingredients, but try to rely mainly on the items you've been given.

Success in the Mystery Ingredient Challenge comes down to a few important tips. First, always taste and adjust flavors as you cook. This helps you balance sweetness, saltiness, and acidity. For example, if your dish is too sour, a bit of sugar can help balance it out. Next, think about the textures and colors in your dish. A good balance of crunchy and soft, as well as vibrant colors, makes your dish more appealing. Finally, keep your dish simple but creative. Sometimes the best dishes are the ones that highlight the natural flavors of the ingredients without overcomplicating things.

Let's look at some example challenges to get you started. Imagine you have apples, cheddar cheese, and tortillas. You could create a sweet and savory quesadilla by slicing the apples thinly, layering them with cheddar cheese on a tortilla, and cooking it until the cheese melts and the tortilla is crispy. Another fun combo is carrots, peanut butter, and rice. Try making a peanut butter stir-fry by sautéing the carrots with some soy sauce, then mixing in cooked rice and a spoonful of peanut butter for a creamy, nutty flavor. For a more adventurous challenge, take spinach, strawberries, and pasta. You could whip up a unique pasta salad by tossing cooked pasta with fresh spinach, sliced strawberries, and a light vinaigrette made from olive oil and lemon juice.

One way to make the Mystery Ingredient Challenge even more engaging is to turn it into a friendly competition. If you have siblings or friends over, divide into teams and see who can come up with the best dish using the same set of ingredients. You can even have a family member act as a judge, scoring the dishes based on creativity, taste, and presentation. This adds an element of excitement and encourages everyone to push their culinary boundaries.

Another tip for success is to use a variety of cooking techniques. For example, you can roast, sauté, or grill your ingredients to bring out different flavors and textures. Experimenting with different methods can lead to surprising and delicious results. Remember, the goal is to have fun and be creative, so don't be afraid to try something new.

The Mystery Ingredient Challenge is a fantastic way to boost your cooking skills and creativity. It teaches you to be resourceful and think on your feet, all while having a great time in the kitchen. So, gather your mystery ingredients, set the timer, and see what delicious creation you can come up with. Happy cooking!

DIY SPICE BLEND CREATIONS

Imagine opening your pantry and finding jars filled with colorful, aromatic spices you made yourself. Creating your own spice blends is not just fun; it's a great way to learn about different spices and how they can transform your dishes. When you make your own spice blends, you get to customize the flavors exactly how you like them. It's like having a magic potion that can make any meal more exciting. Plus, it's a fantastic way to learn about the different spices, their origins, and how they're used in cooking around the world.

Let's start with some basic spice blend recipes that you can easily make at home. First up is Italian Seasoning. This blend is perfect for pasta, pizza, and so many other dishes. Combine one tablespoon each of dried basil, oregano, rosemary, and thyme. Mix them together and store in a small jar. This blend adds a burst of Italian flavor to your meals. Next, we have Taco Seasoning, a must-have for taco nights. Mix together one tablespoon of chili powder, one teaspoon of cumin, one teaspoon of paprika, and one teaspoon of garlic powder. Use this blend to season your meat or veggies for tacos. Finally, let's make Pumpkin Spice, perfect for adding a warm, cozy flavor to your baked goods. Combine one tablespoon each of cinnamon, nutmeg, ginger, and cloves. This blend is great for pumpkin pie, lattes, and even oatmeal.

Creating your own spice blends also allows you to experiment and come up with unique combinations. Start with a base spice, like paprika or cumin, and then add complementary flavors. For example, if you're making a rub for chicken, start with paprika and add some garlic powder, onion powder, and a touch of cayenne for heat. Keep notes on the proportions you use and any adjustments you make. This way, you can recreate your favorite blends or tweak them to make them even better. Don't be afraid to get creative—you might discover a new favorite flavor combination that you love.

Spice blends are incredibly versatile and can be used in many different ways. Try seasoning roasted vegetables with your homemade Italian seasoning. Simply toss the veggies with a bit of olive oil and a sprinkle of the blend before roasting. The herbs will add a delicious flavor that makes the veggies irresistible. Another great use for spice blends is in marinades and rubs for meats. Mix your taco seasoning with a bit of olive oil and lime juice to create a marinade for chicken or beef. Let the meat soak up the flavors before grilling or baking. You can even sprinkle your spice blends on snacks like popcorn or nuts for a tasty, savory treat.

Imagine you've made a batch of your own taco seasoning. You decide to use it to make a quick and easy dinner. You toss some chicken breasts with the seasoning and a bit of olive oil, then grill them until they're perfectly cooked. The aroma fills the kitchen, and when you take that first bite, the flavors are amazing. The blend of spices adds depth and complexity to the chicken, making it way more exciting than plain grilled chicken. This is the magic of homemade spice blends—they take your cooking to the next level with minimal effort.

Another fun way to use your spice blends is in simple snacks. Try sprinkling some of your Italian seasoning on popcorn for a savory twist. Or mix a bit of your pumpkin spice into yogurt or oatmeal for a cozy, autumnal flavor. The possibilities are endless, and you'll find that having these blends on hand makes it easy to add flavor to your meals and snacks.

Creating your own spice blends not only enhances the flavors of your dishes but also adds variety to your cooking. It's a fun and educational project that allows you to experiment with different spices and discover new flavor combinations. So, grab your spices, mix them up, and start seasoning your meals with your very own homemade blends.

GROWING YOUR OWN HERBS

Imagine having a little garden right at your fingertips, filled with fresh, aromatic herbs you can snip off and use in your cooking. Growing your own herbs is not just a fun project; it's incredibly rewarding. You get to enjoy fresh, homegrown ingredients that make your meals taste amazing. Plus, it teaches you responsibility and patience. Watching your herbs grow from tiny seeds into lush plants is a lesson in care and dedication. It's like having a mini science experiment right in your kitchen or backyard.

Starting your own herb garden is easier than you might think. The first step is choosing herbs that are easy to grow. Basil, parsley, and mint are great options for beginners. They're hardy, grow quickly, and can be used in a variety of dishes. Next, you'll need to select the right containers and soil. Herbs can be grown in pots, window boxes, or even recycled containers like old yogurt cups. Make sure your containers have drainage holes to prevent water from pooling at the bottom. Use good-quality potting soil, which provides the nutrients your herbs need to thrive. Place your containers in a sunny spot, as most herbs love sunlight. Aim for about six hours of sunlight each day. Water your herbs regularly, but be careful not to overwater them. The soil should be moist but not soggy.

Taking care of your herb garden involves a few simple tasks. Watering is crucial. Check the soil daily; if it feels dry to the touch, it's time to water. Early morning or late afternoon are the best times to water your plants, as this helps prevent evaporation. Pruning is also important. Regularly snip off the top leaves of your herbs to encourage new growth and prevent them from becoming leggy. This also gives you a steady supply of fresh herbs for cooking. Protecting your herbs from pests is another key step. Look out for common pests like aphids and spider mites. If you spot any, a gentle spray of water or a natural insecticidal soap can help keep them at bay. Finally, knowing when and how to harvest your herbs ensures they stay healthy and productive. Harvest them in the morning after the dew has dried but before the sun's heat is too intense. Cut the stems just above a leaf node to promote further growth.

Once you've harvested your herbs, the fun part begins—using them in your cooking! Fresh herbs can elevate your dishes in so many ways. Take basil, for example. Its sweet, peppery flavor pairs perfectly with pasta dishes. Toss a handful of fresh basil leaves into your spaghetti sauce, or sprinkle them over a Margherita pizza for a burst of fresh flavor. Mint is another versatile herb. It adds a refreshing touch to both sweet and savory dishes. Blend mint leaves into smoothies for a cool, minty twist, or chop them up and mix them into a fruit salad. You can even use mint to make a soothing herbal tea. Parsley, with its bright, slightly peppery taste, is fantastic as a garnish. Sprinkle chopped parsley over soups, salads, or roasted vegetables to add color and a fresh, vibrant flavor.

Growing your own herbs is not just about the end result; it's about the process. It's a chance to connect with nature, learn about plant care, and enjoy the fruits of your labor. There's something incredibly satisfying about snipping off a few fresh herbs and knowing they came from your own garden. It adds a personal touch to your cooking and makes your meals taste even better. So, grab some pots, soil, and seeds, and start your herb garden today. You'll be amazed at how these little plants can transform your cooking and bring a bit of green into your life.

PERSONALIZED RECIPE CARDS

Imagine flipping through a stack of recipe cards filled with your favorite dishes, each one uniquely decorated and personalized. Creating personalized recipe cards is not just a fun project; it's a fantastic way to get organized in the kitchen. It's like making a mini cookbook that's all your own, filled with the recipes you love the most. This project encourages creativity and organization, helping you keep track of your culinary adventures and making it easy to recreate your favorite dishes. Plus, it's a great way to collect and share family recipes, turning your kitchen into a hub of creativity and deliciousness.

To get started, you'll need to decide whether you want to use a template or design your recipe cards from scratch. Templates can be found online and are a great option if you want a polished, uniform look. But designing from scratch allows you to add a personal touch to each card. Once you've decided, gather some index cards or cardstock, colorful pens, and any decorating supplies you might want to use. Each card should include sections for the recipe name, ingredients, instructions, and notes. This helps keep everything clear and organized, making it easy to follow the recipe when you're ready to cook. For example, if you're writing down a recipe for chocolate chip cookies, list the ingredients and their measurements, followed by step-by-step instructions. Leave some space for notes where you can jot down any tweaks or tips for next time.

Next comes the fun part—decorating and personalizing your recipe cards. Use colorful markers to make your cards vibrant and eye-catching. You can draw little illustrations of the ingredients or the finished dish to add a whimsical touch. Stickers are another fun option; they can add a pop of color and personality to your cards. If you're feeling extra creative, you can even add photos of the dish. Simply print out small photos and glue them to the cards. This not only makes your recipe cards look amazing but also gives you a visual reminder of what the dish should look like. Writing special notes or tips on your cards makes them even more personal. For instance, if you've found that adding a pinch of cinnamon to your chocolate chip cookies makes them extra delicious, write that down. These little touches make your recipe cards uniquely yours and a joy to use.

Once you've created your personalized recipe cards, it's important to keep them organized and accessible. A recipe box or binder is a great way to store your cards. You can find decorative recipe boxes that add a touch of charm to your kitchen, or you can use a simple binder with plastic sleeves to protect your cards. Categorizing your recipes by meal type or ingredient makes it easy to find what you're looking for. For example, you can have sections for appetizers, main courses, desserts, and snacks. This way, when you're in the mood to bake cookies or whip up a quick dinner, you can quickly flip to the right section and find the perfect recipe. Regularly updating your collection with new favorite recipes ensures that your recipe box or binder stays fresh and exciting.

Creating personalized recipe cards is a project that combines creativity, organization, and a love for cooking. It's a fun way to document your culinary journey and makes cooking even more enjoyable. You can involve your family or friends in the project, making it a shared experience. Imagine having a collection of beautifully decorated recipe cards that you've created together, each one holding a special memory or a favorite dish. It's not just about the recipes; it's about the joy of creating something meaningful and lasting. So, grab your pens and markers, and start designing your personalized recipe cards today. You'll have a blast creating them, and they'll make your time in the kitchen even more enjoyable.

COOKING WITH LEFTOVERS: CREATIVE IDEAS

Imagine opening your fridge and seeing a mix of leftovers from yesterday's dinner. Instead of letting them go to waste, why not turn them into a new, delicious meal? Cooking with leftovers is not only a great way to reduce food waste but also a fantastic opportunity to get creative in the kitchen. By repurposing leftovers, you save money and make the most out of the food you already have. Plus, it's a fun challenge to see what new dishes you can come up with using what's on hand.

Using leftovers well starts with identifying versatile ingredients that can be transformed into various dishes. For example, cooked rice, roasted vegetables, and chicken are all great base ingredients. Combining these leftovers helps create balanced meals that are both tasty and nutritious. Leftover rice can be turned into a flavorful stir-fry by sautéing it with some mixed vegetables and a splash of soy sauce. Roasted vegetables can be added to a salad or blended into a soup. Leftover chicken can be shredded and used in tacos, sandwiches, or even a hearty chicken salad.

One creative way to use leftover rice is to make a stir-fry. Heat some oil in a pan and add any leftover veggies you have on hand—carrots, bell peppers, and peas work great. Sauté them until they're tender, then add the leftover rice and a splash of soy sauce. Stir everything together until it's heated through. You can also add a scrambled egg or some cooked shrimp for extra protein. This quick and easy dish transforms your leftover rice into a delicious new meal.

If you have leftover roast chicken, why not turn it into a fresh and tasty salad? Start by shredding the chicken and mixing it with some greens like spinach or lettuce. Add in some sliced cucumbers, cherry tomatoes, and perhaps a handful of nuts for crunch. For the dressing, a simple mix of olive oil, lemon juice, salt, and pepper works wonderfully. Toss everything together, and you have a light and satisfying meal that's perfect for lunch or dinner.

Mashed potatoes from last night's dinner can be turned into crispy, golden patties. Combine the leftover mashed potatoes with a beaten egg and some breadcrumbs to form a dough. Shape the mixture into small patties and fry them in a bit of oil until they're crispy on the outside and soft on the inside. These patties make a fantastic side dish or a fun snack. You can even add some cheese or herbs to the mixture for extra flavor.

Properly storing and reheating leftovers is crucial to maintain their quality and ensure they're safe to eat. Use airtight containers to store your leftovers. This helps keep them fresh and prevents any odors from spreading in the fridge. Label each container with the date, so you know how long the leftovers have been stored. Most leftovers are best consumed within three to four days. When reheating, do so gently to avoid drying out the food. For dishes like stir-fries or pasta, a quick zap in the microwave with a splash of water can help restore moisture. For items like chicken or potato patties, reheating them in the oven can help keep their texture intact.

Cooking with leftovers encourages you to be resourceful and inventive. It's a great way to experiment with flavors and textures without the pressure of following a strict recipe. Plus, it's incredibly satisfying to turn something that might have been thrown away into a delicious, new dish. So next time you open your fridge and see leftovers, think of it as an opportunity to create something amazing. You'll not only enjoy a tasty meal but also do your part in reducing food waste.

CHAPTER 10

Seasonal and Special Recipes

Picture this: It's a sweltering summer afternoon, and you're lounging in the backyard with your friends. The sun is blazing, and everyone is craving something cold and refreshing. Now imagine heading inside and whipping up some homemade popsicles that are bursting with flavor and coolness. Making popsicles at home is not only a fun and refreshing summer activity but also incredibly easy with just a few simple ingredients.

SUMMER POPSICLES AND COOL TREATS

Homemade popsicles are the perfect way to cool down on hot summer days, and the best part is that you can create them with ingredients you probably already have at home. You don't need special equipment—just a blender and some popsicle molds or even small paper cups with wooden sticks. Popsicles are versatile and can be as simple or as creative as you like. Fresh fruit, juice, and yogurt are your main ingredients, and from there, the sky's the limit.

To start with a basic popsicle recipe, gather your ingredients: fresh fruit, juice, and yogurt. For a straightforward fruit popsicle, blend one cup of fresh or frozen fruit with half a cup of juice and half a cup of yogurt until smooth. You can use any fruit you like—strawberries, blueberries, mangoes, or a mix. Pour the blended mixture into popsicle molds, insert the sticks, and freeze for at least four hours or until they are completely solid. If you don't have molds, use small paper cups and cover them with foil before inserting the sticks. This keeps the sticks upright while the popsicles freeze.

Now, let's get creative with some unique popsicle variations that will make your taste buds dance. Berry Lemonade Pops are a delightful mix of tart and sweet. Blend mixed berries with lemonade for a refreshing twist. For a tropical vibe, try Tropical Paradise Pops. Blend mango, pineapple, and coconut milk for a creamy, exotic treat that will transport you to a beachside paradise with every lick. If you're a chocolate lover, Chocolate Banana Pops are a must-try. Blend bananas with cocoa powder and milk for a rich, chocolaty delight. Each variation offers a different flavor experience, and you can customize them to your liking.

To ensure your popsicles turn out delicious and well-formed, here are a few tips. First, use ripe, sweet fruit for the best flavor. If the fruit isn't sweet enough, you can add a little honey or agave to the mixture. This natural sweetness enhances the fruit flavors and makes the popsicles even more enjoyable. Second, make sure to blend the mixture until it's very smooth. This helps the popsicles freeze evenly and gives them a nice, creamy texture. Third, freeze the popsicles for at least four hours or until they are completely solid. This ensures they hold their shape and don't melt too quickly once you take them out of the molds.

For an interactive element, consider creating a popsicle-making station at your next summer gathering. Set out bowls of different fruits, juices, yogurts, and sweeteners, and let everyone create their own custom popsicles. This not only makes the process fun but also allows everyone to experiment with different flavor combinations. You can even have a taste-testing session once the popsicles are frozen to see which combination is the most popular.

POPSICLE-MAKING CHECKLIST

- Fresh or frozen fruit (e.g., strawberries, blueberries, mangoes)
- Juice (e.g., lemonade, orange juice, apple juice)
- Yogurt (Greek or regular)
- Sweeteners (honey or agave, optional)
- Blender
- Popsicle molds or small paper cups
- Wooden sticks

Using this checklist ensures you have everything you need for a successful popsicle-making session.

Making popsicles at home is a fun, easy, and rewarding activity that brings a burst of flavor to hot summer days. Whether you're enjoying a Berry Lemonade Pop by the pool, savoring a Tropical Paradise Pop while lounging in the hammock, or indulging in a Chocolate Banana Pop after a day of fun in the sun, these homemade treats are sure to become a summer favorite.

COZY WINTER SOUPS

Imagine coming home on a chilly winter day, your cheeks rosy from the cold, and being greeted by the comforting aroma of a hearty soup simmering on the stove. Winter soups have a special charm, providing warmth and nourishment when the weather is harsh. They wrap you in a cozy embrace, making you feel all warm and fuzzy inside. Not only do they warm you up, but they're also packed with nutrients, making them a perfect meal for those cold days. Plus, soups are incredibly easy to make in large batches, which means you can enjoy them for several days or even freeze some for later.

Making a basic winter soup is simpler than you might think. You'll need some key ingredients: broth, root vegetables, protein (like beans or chicken), and herbs. Start by sautéing your veggies. In a large pot, heat a little oil and add chopped onions, carrots, and celery. These three form the base of many soups and are often called the "holy trinity" of soup making. Cook them until they're soft and fragrant. Then, add your broth. You can use chicken, beef, or vegetable broth, depending on your preference. Next, toss in your protein. If you're using chicken, it's best to add it raw and let it cook in the soup. If you're using beans, you can add them straight from the can (just make sure to rinse them first). Finally, add some herbs for flavor. Bay leaves, thyme, and rosemary work well. Let everything simmer together until the flavors meld and the ingredients are cooked through.

Now, let's explore some creative winter soup recipes that will make your taste buds sing. First up is a Creamy Potato Soup. This soup is rich and velvety, perfect for those who love a creamy texture. Start with the basics: sauté onions and leeks in butter until they're soft. Add diced potatoes and enough chicken broth to cover them. Let the potatoes cook until they're tender. Then, using an immersion blender, blend the soup until smooth. Stir in some crispy bacon bits and shredded cheddar cheese for a delicious finish.

Next, we have a Hearty Beef Stew. This soup is more like a meal in itself, packed with chunks of tender beef, carrots, potatoes, and peas. Begin by browning beef chunks in a pot. This step adds depth of flavor. Once the beef is browned, remove it from the pot and sauté onions, carrots, and celery. Add the beef back in along with beef broth, diced potatoes, and peas. Let everything simmer until the beef is tender and the vegetables are cooked through. This stew is perfect for a cold winter night, filling you up and keeping you warm.

For something a bit different, try a Spiced Lentil Soup. This soup is hearty and packed with flavor, thanks to the addition of spices like cumin and turmeric. Start by sautéing onions, garlic, and ginger in a pot. Add diced tomatoes and cook until they're soft. Then, add lentils, vegetable broth, and a combination of spices (cumin, turmeric, and a pinch of chili powder). Let the lentils cook until they're tender. Stir in some fresh spinach just before serving for a pop of color and added nutrition.

To ensure your soups turn out rich and flavorful, here are a few tips. First, use homemade broth whenever possible. It adds a depth of flavor that store-bought broth can't match. If you don't have homemade broth, you can enhance store-bought broth by simmering it with extra veggies and herbs for a while before using it in your soup. Second, let your soup simmer slowly. This allows the flavors to develop and meld together beautifully. The longer it simmers, the better it will taste. Finally, don't forget the garnishes. A sprinkle of fresh herbs like parsley or cilantro, a dollop of cream, or a handful of croutons can elevate your soup and make it even more delicious.

Consider creating a winter soup night with your friends or family. Set up a soup bar with different toppings and garnishes, and let everyone customize their bowls to their liking. You could even try making all three of these soups and having a taste-test to see which one is the favorite. This not only makes for a fun and interactive meal but also showcases the versatility and deliciousness of winter soups.

FESTIVE HOLIDAY COOKIES

Imagine it's the holiday season, the air is filled with the scent of pine and cinnamon, and the kitchen is buzzing with excitement. Baking holiday cookies is one of the most fun and festive activities you can do during this time of year. It's not just about the delicious treats you'll get to eat; it's also about the joy of creating something beautiful and sharing it with others. Holiday cookies make perfect gifts, and they can be a delightful way to show someone you care. Plus, decorating cookies encourages creativity, turning your kitchen into a mini art studio.

Let's start with a simple recipe for classic sugar cookie dough. You'll need some basic ingredients: flour, sugar, butter, eggs, and vanilla extract. Begin by creaming together one cup of softened butter with one cup of sugar until the mixture is light and fluffy. This usually takes about two to three minutes using an electric mixer. Next, add in one large egg and one teaspoon of vanilla extract, and mix until well combined. In a separate bowl, whisk together three cups of flour with half a teaspoon of baking powder. Gradually add the dry ingredients to the wet ingredients, mixing just until the dough comes together. Once your dough is ready, wrap it in plastic wrap and chill it in the refrigerator for at least an hour. Chilling the dough makes it easier to roll out and helps the cookies hold their shape better during baking.

After the dough has chilled, it's time to roll it out and cut it into shapes. Lightly flour your work surface and rolling pin to prevent sticking. Roll the dough to about a quarter-inch thickness, making sure it's even for consistent baking. Use cookie cutters to cut out festive shapes like snowflakes, reindeer, and stars. Place the cut-out cookies on a baking sheet lined with parchment paper, leaving a little space between each one. Bake the cookies in a preheated oven at 350°F (175°C) for about 10-12 minutes, or until the edges are just starting to turn golden. Let the cookies cool completely on a wire rack before you start decorating.

Now comes the fun part: decorating your holiday cookies. There are so many ways to get creative with your designs. One simple way is to use colored icing and sprinkles. You can make a basic icing by mixing powdered sugar with a little milk and food coloring. Use piping bags or squeeze bottles to apply the icing in intricate patterns, and sprinkle on some colorful sprinkles while the icing is still wet. Another fun idea is to add edible glitter and decorative candies. These can make your cookies sparkle and shine, adding an extra festive touch. You can also create themed cookies by using different colors and designs. For example, use white and blue icing to make snowflakes, red and green for Christmas trees, or brown and white for gingerbread men.

To make sure your holiday cookies turn out beautifully decorated and delicious, here are a few tips. First, roll the dough evenly. This ensures that all your cookies bake at the same rate and prevents some from burning while others are still undercooked. Second, let the cookies cool completely before you start decorating. If the cookies are still warm, the icing can melt and run, ruining your designs. Third, store your decorated cookies in airtight containers to keep them fresh. Layer them with parchment paper to prevent the decorations from smudging, and keep them in a cool, dry place.

For an interactive element, consider hosting a cookie decorating party with your friends or family. Set up a decorating station with various icings, sprinkles, and candies. Provide each guest with a batch of plain cookies and let them unleash their creativity. This not only makes for a fun and festive activity but also allows everyone to take home a box of beautifully decorated cookies. You can even have a friendly competition to see who can create the most impressive designs.

Baking holiday cookies is more than just making tasty treats. It's about the experience of creating something special, the joy of sharing it with loved ones, and the fun of letting your creativity shine. So, gather your ingredients, preheat the oven, and get ready to fill your home with the delicious aroma and festive spirit of holiday cookies.

Conclusion

Wow, young chefs! Can you believe how far you've come? From learning the basics of kitchen safety to whipping up delicious dishes, you've embarked on an incredible culinary journey. Remember the first time you cracked an egg or chopped a vegetable? It might have seemed daunting at first, but look at you now! You've not only learned how to cook but also discovered the joy and creativity that come with it. You've made smoothie bowls, baked cookies, and even tackled dinner dishes that would make any chef proud. Give yourselves a pat on the back because you've earned it!

Throughout this cookbook, we've covered a lot of ground. We started with the essentials, ensuring you knew how to stay safe and use your kitchen tools properly. Then, we dove into breakfast delights, showing you how to make everything from fluffy pancakes to vibrant smoothie bowls. We explored creative snacks that are both tasty and nutritious, perfect for after-school munchies. Lunches became exciting with sandwich wraps and bento boxes, while dinners turned into a delightful experience with one-pot meals and build-your-own tacos. We also embraced the fun of making sweet treats and celebrated the joy of cooking with seasonal and special recipes.

But beyond the recipes and techniques, there are a few key takeaways I'd like you to remember. First, cooking is about creativity. It's about experimenting with flavors, trying new ingredients, and making each dish your own. Don't be afraid to tweak recipes to suit your taste. Second, cooking brings people together. Whether you're making a meal for your family, having a pizza night with friends, or hosting a cookie decorating party, food has a unique way of creating memories and strengthening bonds. Finally, cooking is a skill that grows with you. The more you practice, the more confident and skilled you'll become.

Now that you've mastered these recipes and techniques, it's time to take the next step. Keep exploring new recipes, watch cooking shows, and read other cookbooks. Share your newfound skills with others by cooking for your family and friends. Don't hesitate to experiment and create your own recipes. And remember, cooking isn't just about following instructions; it's about expressing yourself and having fun.

As you continue on your culinary journey, there will be times when things don't go as planned. Maybe a dish doesn't turn out the way you expected, or you accidentally burn something. That's okay! Mistakes are part of the learning process. Each time you face a challenge in the kitchen, you gain valuable experience that makes you a better cook. Embrace every mistake as a learning opportunity and keep pushing forward.

Cooking is a lifelong adventure filled with endless possibilities. There's always something new to learn, a new recipe to try, or a new technique to master. So, keep your curiosity alive and never stop exploring. Your kitchen is your playground, and the world of food is vast and exciting. Whether you're cooking a simple breakfast or a fancy dinner, remember to enjoy every moment.

Thank you for allowing me to be a part of your culinary journey. It's been a joy guiding you through these recipes and watching you grow as a young chef. Keep cooking, keep experimenting, and most importantly, keep having fun in the kitchen. The skills and memories you've gained from this cookbook are just the beginning. The world is your oyster, and I can't wait to see what delicious creations you'll come up with next. Happy cooking!

References

- *Kitchen Safety for Kids | UNL Food* https://food.unl.edu/newsletter/food-fun-young-children/kitchen-safety-rules-kids
- *The Best Kids Cooking Tools (That You'll Love Too)* https://www.nytimes.com/wirecutter/reviews/best-tools-for-cooking-with-kids/
- *The Easiest Recipes and Techniques for Beginner Cooks* https://www.eater.com/2020/4/3/21203517/easy-cooking-recipes-tips-tricks-roast-chicken-vegetables-rice-beans
- *Kids in the Kitchen- Measuring Techniques* https://www.landolakes.com/expert-advice/kids-in-the-kitchen-measuring-techniques/
- *Berry Smoothie Bowl (to Share with the Kids)* https://www.yummytoddlerfood.com/berry-smoothie-bowls-for-the-whole-family/
- *Benefits of Oats + Overnight Oats for Kids* https://plantbasedjuniors.com/benefits-of-oats-overnight-oats-for-kids/

- *20 Irresistibly Cute Pancake Ideas For Kids -* https://helloyummy.co/cute-pancake-ideas-for-kids/
- *What are some good fillings to put in a breakfast burrito that ...* https://www.quora.com/What-are-some-good-fillings-to-put-in-a-breakfast-burrito-that-are-not-eggs-or-bacon-sausage
- *The Surprising Benefits of Green Vegetables For Kids* https://hiyahealth.com/blogs/news/the-surprising-benefits-of-green-vegetables-for-kids#:~:text=The%20benefits%20of%20green%20leafy,helping%20to%20reduce%20unhealthy%20snacking.
- *31 Dips and Dippable Snack Recipes Kids Will Love* https://www.epicurious.com/recipes-menus/kid-approved-after-school-snacks-for-dipping-gallery
- *Easy Kid's Trail Mix Recipe* https://www.momentswithmandi.com/easy-kids-trail-mix-recipe/
- *No-Bake Energy Bites Recipe* https://www.allrecipes.com/recipe/239969/no-bake-energy-bites/
- *Wraps for Kids: 10 Easy Ideas for Lunch or Dinner* https://www.yummytoddlerfood.com/wraps-for-kids/
- *62 Brilliant Bento Box Lunch Ideas for Kids (Picky Eater ...* https://twomamabears.com/brilliant-bento-box-lunch-ideas-for-kids-picky-eater-friendly/

- *10 Allergy-Free School Lunch Box Ideas for Kids* https://babyfoode.com/blog/10-allergy-friendly-school-lunches-nut-free-dairy-free-gluten-free/
- *4 Soup Recipes Your Kids Can Make* https://countryhomelearningcenter.com/4-soup-recipes-kids-can-make/
- *Mini Pizza Bites – Fun and Easy Cooking with Kids* https://www.muminthemadhouse.com/mini-pizza-bites-cooking-with-kids/
- *Healthy Nachos {With Veggies & Kid Friendly!}* https://foodplaygo.com/2020/08/21/healthy-nachos-with-veggies-kid-friendly/
- *Delicious and Kid-Friendly: 5 Quesadilla Combinations ...* https://medina.macaronikid.com/articles/65d795c79d6c013d6e85015e/delicious-and-kid-friendly-5-quesadilla-combinations-theyll-love
- *Sweet N' Salty Party Popcorn* https://pintsizedbaker.com/sweet-n-salty-party-popcorn/
- *One Pot Meals: Highly Recommended For Children* https://mydaughtersandme.com/one-pot-meals-highly-recommended-for-children/
- *How to Build the Ultimate Taco Bar* https://www.food.com/how-to/build-the-ultimate-taco-bar-202
- *Easy Vegetable Stir Fry* https://www.budgetbytes.com/easy-vegetable-stir-fry/
- *Sheet Pan Chicken with Rainbow Vegetables* https://www.wellplated.com/sheet-pan-chicken-rainbow-vegetables/

- *How to Make an Irresistible Ice Cream Sundae Bar* https://www.tasteofhome.com/article/how-to-make-an-ice-cream-sundae-bar/
- *Tori Avey's Easy Homemade Tutorial: Chocolate ...* https://toriavey.com/chocolate-dipped-strawberries/
- *15 No-Bake Cookies to Make With Your Kids* https://www.allrecipes.com/gallery/easy-cookie-recipes-for-kids/
- *Funfetti Cupcakes Recipe* https://www.bostongirlbakes.com/funfetti-cupcakes-recipe/
- *The 10 Best Sliders for Kids (Quick and Simple!)* https://platein28.com/sliders-for-kids/
- *Crudite Platter: Elegant Veggie Tray Ideas* https://ainttooproudtomeg.com/elevated-veggie-platter/
- *How To Host A Make Your Own Pizza Party* https://natalieparamore.com/how-to-host-a-make-your-own-pizza-party/
- *28 Non-Alcoholic Punch Recipes* https://www.southernliving.com/food/drinks/non-alcoholic-punch-recipes
- *10 kids' cooking projects* https://www.bbcgoodfood.com/howto/guide/10-kids-cooking-projects-you-should-be-doing-half-term
- *Chopped Mystery Basket Ideas for Middle School and High ...* https://twinsandteaching.com/2021/11/16/mystery-basket-chopped-activity-for-middle-and-high-school/

- *Kids In The Kitchen: Homemade Spice Blend Recipes* https://areasonforhomeschool.com/kids-in-the-kitchen-homemade-spice-blend-recipes/
- *Growing Herbs with Children* https://www.kidsdogardening.com/growing-herbs-with-children/
- *How to Make Popsicles (Ultimate Guide)* https://www.yummytoddlerfood.com/how-to-make-popsicles/
- *15+ Easy Winter Soup Recipes for Dinner - EatingWell* https://www.eatingwell.com/gallery/7938033/easy-winter-soup-recipes-for-dinner/
- *Easy Decorated Christmas Cookies (aka A Snowy ...* https://thecafesucrefarine.com/easy-decorated-christmas-cookies/
- *How to Make Popsicles (Ultimate Guide)* https://www.yummytoddlerfood.com/how-to-make-popsicles/

www.ingramcontent.com/pod-product-compliance
Lightning Source LLC
Chambersburg PA
CBHW072228150726
48002CB00005B/1978